FINDING THE FAIRWAY
A Journey To The Game of Golf
By
Lee Wood

Table of Contents

Why Golf?

I almost hesitate to write on the subject at all. I am one of the many whose enthusiasm by no means creates great play. I am not only a bad golfer, but I have the unhappy and well-grounded conviction that I shall always remain a bad golfer. It seems to me something like impertinence then to write on the subject at all. I only do so because I want to impress upon others the conviction I have myself that golf can be immensely enjoyed even by bad players and by players who have started it – like me – late in life.

The curious charm of golf is independent of your skill. Golf is not like other games or sports where your lack of ability injures not only yourself but also your partner.

Something else I am very fond of doing is playing cards, but I play cards only when I have partners who have a good temperament and a bad memory. Nothing in the world would induce me to play cards with an opponent who could play a good game but had a bad temper. You rarely, if ever, have such an experience in golf. It is the most good-natured game in the world. The whole tone is to encourage your partner. I have never heard one golfer yell "Lousy shot!" after his partner has hit a bad one, but I have often heard a golfer make that observation about his own shot coupled with expletives that added force and picturesque-ness to the observation. On the contrary, if you hit an errant shot, your playing partner often says the shot "will work" or convincingly comment "what rotten luck" – the point being that it is not you who are at fault. This spirit of geniality that you find among golfers extends to every player, regardless of skill level. Unfortunately, many playing partners comment "great shot" just as the ball leaves the club-face when where the ball ends up is still yet to be determined. This is what you would call "getting the compliment out of the way so I can focus on my own shot."

One of the things that strike the non-golfer is the extraordinary fascination the game exercises over its devotees. For example, after men have played golf all day, they are quite ready to talk about golf all night. There are plenty of men known to all of us who are ready to travel from one end of the country to the other to play good links. Vacations are even arranged by most golfers with a view to play golf and nothing would induce the majority of them to go anywhere if they were not assured of getting in a round.

I always try to get at the psychology of any human pursuit and I have done my best to analyze the emotions that account for the fascination of golf. I think I have managed to find them out. The first attraction of course is the fact that golf takes you out into the open air and makes it agreeable to remain there. The longer I live, the more faith I have in open air and the more I resent the amount of energy, spirit and effectiveness that is destroyed by living our lives without ventilation. Out there on the links, we experience a modicum of freedom. Who could not be attracted to that?

The next explanation for the fascination of golf is that it is a sport that can be taken up at any age. You can walk either quickly or slowly - exactly as you feel inclined. In golf, the better practice is to walk slowly rather than quickly but for the group behind you it is better to walk quickly rather than slowly.

The other benefit of golf is that it can be played any time of the year (at least somewhere in the world) with almost as much enjoyment in winter as in summer and although the golfer is not independent of weather, he is often indifferent to it. I have frequently seen golfers playing in the rain. I myself have done this. I have even played in a bad fog and the best proof that snow is of no concern to the golfer is the fact that there is a special ball for playing in the snow – the ball is red instead of white.

Compare golf to any other outdoor game and the first advantage you will see is that in golf you can play by yourself and still get the full experience and satisfaction of the game. Of course you won't have a witness to your hole-in-one, but that is not a high likelihood anyway.

You can't properly play football or tennis with yourself. Besides, golf depends mainly on you. In other sports, whether or not you are going to score depends on so many people outside of yourself. In golf there is no such divided responsibility. There is the ball, there are your clubs; whether you make a good shot or a bad shot is your affair and nobody else's business. You may have your bits of bad luck; your ball may hit a tree or fall in a ditch or just stop short of a hole, but these are circumstances with which every golfer has to contend. The main thing is that you must play your stroke well yourself and that means that you are to fall back on phrases like "I am the captain of my own soul, the master of my own destiny, the maker of my own luck" – crap like that.

Each shot that a golfer plays has its own history, its own drama. You hit the ball squarely and fairly or you hit the ball half squarely or half fairly or you hit the ball badly or you miss it altogether. There is a whole set of possibilities that await every golfer when he or she starts to hit the ball. The ball speeds on its course and again another new set of infinite possibilities arise. The ball may keep straight on the course and then its destination is clear. Or, the ball may go out of bounds and then the stroke is lost. Or, the ball may get into long grass and then there is a difficulty in getting it out again. Think of all the possibilities!

If you really want to understand the perplexities and possibilities of each stroke in a golf match you ought to play golf with a seasoned Scottish caddie attending you. They rush after the ball, then they stand looking at it for several seconds and it is not until they have fully pondered the ball's situation that they then advise you which of your clubs you should attempt to use.

I may be accused of painting a false picture when I say that each stroke is a drama but this gives you some idea why golf is so fascinating. I count it among the beneficent revolutions and revelations of our time (especially for middle-aged men of sedentary employment).

I have made numerous converts from all types of professions. Their gratitude to me for introducing them to the game of golf, however, does not prevent them from cursing me for getting them into the game and it does not prevent them from becoming better players in a month than I could succeed in being in a year.

But the joy of golf does not wholly depend on success.

*

The above was written by T.P. O'Connor at the turn of the 20th century and his words still ring true today in the year 2013. Every day somewhere in the world another person discovers the game and their obsession with golf begins.

No one gets to the game of golf without the influence or inspiration of someone else. This book chronicles my personal journey to the game of golf but before I even held a club in my hand, my interest in golf was sustained by the characters and events in the golf world. I have recounted those stories in this book because they are the stories that inspired, influenced and motivated me to pursue the game. They are not in chronological order because learning about golf is a process of looking at the present and of looking back at its history. Contrary to the opinion of some non-golfers, golf is not a selfish game. It is a game that is shared from person to person and generation to generation.

Because when we share our experiences, we just may inspire someone else.

CHAPTER ONE

Visions of Green

November 18, 2013, Blackhorse course at Bayonet/Blackhorse, Seaside California. The second hole is a very long 247 yards (from the back tee) par 3 with a deep green where the front of the green is uphill but the back of the green slopes downhill with a dramatic drop-off to the left. The pin was in the back center so that drop-off was definitely in play. My playing partners Plaxton and Joe hit short of the green and in the left rough, respectively. I hit my tee shot on the right edge of the green but had a long 30-foot uphill putt that broke dramatically left.

Plax and Joe chipped up to the green, but their shots fell away. I patiently studied my putt as they both hit their third shots within a few feet of the hole and marked their balls for bogie attempts.

I was ready. I saw the line. Yes indeed I saw that line. Taking back my 34 inch putter, I stroked it perfectly and watched as it climbed the hill and then broke left travelling at a decent clip until it plopped right into the middle of the hole. A thrill shot through me. I'd made a birdie and in dramatic fashion. Fist bumps all around.

That jolt was one of the reasons I played golf and why I kept coming back, but golf is more than a game. For me, golf has always been a lifeline.

*

Phil Mickelson is quoted as saying that he was dreaming about golf before he even learned to walk.

As far back as I can remember, even when I was being pushed around in a stroller, I had flashing "visions" of swinging a golf club. As I grew up, I constantly thought about golf, talked about golf, read about golf and dreamed about playing golf.

Golf played a big role in the country where I was born and raised, South Africa. We lived in Durban, a beautiful bustling city that sits on the edge of the warm Indian Ocean. Durban is famous for being the busiest port in South Africa and the continent of Africa and is a popular tourist destination because of the warm subtropical climate and extensive beaches. Our high-rise apartment, modern but not fancy, was several blocks away from The Durban Golf Club.

The club was first established in 1892 after a local bank manager approached the town council about creating a golf club in Durban. He was granted permission to lay out a links design course on the grounds. The first course was a far cry from the professionally landscaped grounds of today. There were no actual greens – only scuffed ground with hard clay surfaces and the fairways were not planted. The grass was merely cut by a reaper drawn by oxen.

In 1932, the Durban Golf Club was rebuilt. A brand new clubhouse replaced the original wood and iron shanty, and a new course layout was designed by Bob Grimsdell. Considered one of the proudest moments in the history of the club was on April 8, 1932 when (following a visit from Edward VIII, the then-Prince of Wales, in 1925) Durban Golf Club was granted permission to use the prefix "Royal" by King George V, making it one of only four golf clubs in southern Africa to obtain this honor. It was at this time that the Royal Durban Golf Club also designed and introduced their club badge, which is still used today. The motto "Ludus

Palma Potior" has been officially translated as "the game supersedes the man."

The Royal Durban Golf Club was one of the very few golf courses to be situated in the middle of a horse racing track and has hosted some renowned golfing tournaments in the last 100 years, including the South African Championship in 1911 and the Commonwealth Tournament in 1975 which saw Nick Faldo playing at the age of eighteen.

The Greyville Racecourse had hosted numerous prestigious racing events. My paternal grandfather owned thoroughbred race horses and they frequently raced at Greyville. Though I love horses, I was more interested in checking out the golf course when we went to the track.

My earliest memory of seeing the golf course was as a toddler sitting in a stroller and pointing at it. I was fidgety, fussing to get a closer look. I was like a missile locked on a target. I then felt a sharp pain course through my arm. I stopped fussing and stared at the course with fascination, rubbing my sore arm.

As the years passed, every racing weekend I was eager to return to the Greyville Racecourse just so that I could see the Royal Durban Golf Club. It seemed like the most special and secretive place in the world. I still had not seen a full view of the course, just snippets here and there through the bushes. Sunny skies seemed to illuminate the course, highlighting every undulation. Cloudy days seemed to shroud the course in mystery.

One day when I was about eight years old, I asked my mother if I could go see the course up close, if perhaps I could even play golf (though I had no real concept of the game). I winced as that sharp pain coursed through my arm.

"Don't be ridiculous," she said.

I watched her leave, rubbing my upper arm where she had pinched it. My arm was sore, always sore, from her pinching it, but I was soon distracted. I noticed a weak area in the fence. I ran over, fell to my belly and crawled under that section of the fence to where I could just pop my head out onto the golf course. I hid each time a player came close to me, but otherwise, I watched the players come through one by one. Men were out there playing what appeared to be the most fun game in the entire world. Hitting a ball with a funny shaped stick and watching that ball fly onto (not always) the green. From then on, I desperately wanted to play golf.

When I returned to the racetrack that day, my parents and paternal grandparents stood grouped together, frowning.

"Where were you?" Dad demanded. "You little twerp!"

I was scared, trying to respond but nothing would come out of my mouth. Mom leaned over to me. The pain coursed through my arm.

Grandma bent down, her expensive cologne mingling with the vodka on her breath as she put her arm around me. "Where were you, darling?" she asked.

I relished the sensation of her holding me. It was a rare and special thing. I touched her arm, the fine texture of her custom-tailored jacket beneath my fingers. She seemed too clean and perfect to touch.

"I saw the golf," I said. "I want to play."

She laughed, stumbled back, unsteady. "Oh you silly child!"

"Impertinent child more like it," Grandpa barked.

A strict disciplinarian with a hair-trigger temper that he had passed on to my father, I then learned that Grandpa was intolerant about the subject of golf. He sternly expressed to me that golf was a complete and utter waste of time – a game for slackers, loafers and fancy boys. Mom and Dad echoed his sentiments. The pain coursed through my arm. I was embarrassed for suggesting such an onerous thing and humiliated for being scolded in public.

On the ride back to our apartment, I knew I was going to get a hiding (that's what we called a spanking in South Africa) for disappearing like that and I was scared. I had lost all sense of time lying there on my belly watching the golf. As scared as I was about being hit when we got home, I was more upset about being told that golf was a bad thing.

My parents and grandparents were not the only ones who looked down their noses at golf. The game had sparked controversy when golf first took hold in England. The former Prime Minister of the United Kingdom, Arthur Balfour, even made a speech promoting golf to combat the negativity. He was of the opinion that the game was an important factor in making life pleasant and healthy. The multiplication of golf courses in neighborhoods of crowded business centers had greatly increased the amenities of life for many Balfour argued. He and a rising number of golf enthusiasts all across the world denied that golf was idle folly and touted the health benefits of the game.

"The pursuit of health can never be a waste of time," he declared.

Yet, in those early days, it was still the opinion of many that the Scottish national game was nothing but a waste of time. Time spent over golf, the critics said, would be better spent on more serious matters. Touting the physical benefits of golf could never substitute for the time it takes away from what people should be doing. The critics argued that whatever is worth doing is worth doing well and no one can play golf really well without devoting an inordinate amount of time to the game.

Even newspapers around the country began to debate the issue. What should the common man do? Should he quit playing a game in which he can only excel at by the expenditure of much time? Should he play moderately well but lament that he could play better if only he had more time? Or, should he give more thought to serious matters and abandon this sport of laborious idleness?

For me, there was no option but one. I was to abandon any thought of playing golf.

"You must think you can live a life of luxury playing golf while the rest of us work," Mom said, her shrill voice piercing my ear drum as pain coursed through my arm.

I knew that I still worked hard on my school work even though I dreamed about playing golf, but I would not dare argue that point with her.

School was in the opposite direction of the Royal Durban Golf Club, so I never got to peer over the fence at the fairways and greens when I walked to school or else I would have left at least an hour earlier so I could watch the early birds take to the course.

School was a significant distance from our apartment and I ran into more than one mysterious stranger trying to lure me into his car or apartment but I always ran away in fear. Durban was big and beautiful, but it had its share of underworld darkness and increasing racial tension. Each day it seemed the city was getter darker, grittier, a more dangerous place.

At my school, going out for sports was not a choice. You didn't go out for the team. You were on the team. We were broken up either into the A, B, C or D team based on athletic ability. The A Team consisted of stellar athletes and was the team that represented the school in major competitions. It was a great way of including all kids in sports – no one was left out unless severely physically disabled.

I was on the C Team, athletic enough but I petered out over the long haul due to lack of stamina. We mostly did Olympic style events such as track and field, shot put and long jump. None of these interested me that much and there was no golf program.

Outside of school, the major sporting activity in Durban was surfing. My older brother, Tay, surfed and I would tag along with his group of friends, but I wouldn't take on the big waves. It was easy to learn surfing when I was young and flexible. The warm Indian Ocean made going out even more enjoyable. However, surfing did not excite me enough to replace my interest in golf. On the beach I found a nice piece of driftwood that had been rolled smooth by the tide, perhaps over many years, and it made for an acceptable club. At a relatively secluded spot I hit rocks and shells into the ocean – secluded so I wouldn't shank a shell in someone's eye (which I unfortunately discovered does happen). With my bare feet on the hot sand, it was a fun task for me to try to launch the rocks into the sea.

Despite the numerous outdoor activities available to me in the seaside city of Durban, my "visions" of playing golf continued. I began to question them and feel frustrated by them. Why were those "visions" always there? I hadn't played golf before, not even held a golf club, so where did the visions come from? And exactly who was I to even have a vision about playing golf anyway? Visions like that belonged to people who were actually in the game, who played or competed at a high level. I was just a little pipsqueak.

A pro golfer like Johnny Miller had earned the right to have visions. In fact, he said that when he was standing on the 15th tee at the 1971 Masters Tournament, he suddenly had a vision that he was wearing the green jacket. He had the lead over Jack Nicklaus, Arnold Palmer and his friend Billy Casper, who had called Miller "the greatest newcomer to the tour."

The vision Miller had of himself wearing the green jacket was not a delusion, an impossible feat. Nicklaus' game was off because he was having trouble with his putting, so Miller felt he did have a chance to win the event.

Johnny teed off on the final round on Sunday four strokes off the pace. His game heated up that day and he went three under par on the front nine. His good play continued on the back nine when he sank a nine-foot putt for birdie on the 11th hole and chipped out of a bunker for a birdie on the difficult 12th hole. He missed a third birdie on the 13th, but managed to get one on 14. He was now 6 under par and in the lead – no wonder he was having visions of wearing the green jacket.

Prior to that day, Miller had never really imagined winning the tournament. The Masters was stiff competition and to win meant that he was beating the best players in the world. That Sunday he felt loose and free, almost like he was playing a practice round, but at the 15th tee he began to feel the pressure. The 15th hole is steeped in golf lore. That is where Gene Sarazen scored a double eagle (and it is the same hole years later in 2013 when Tiger Woods was penalized for taking an illegal drop).

The 15th hole had changed dramatically since Sarazen's unforgettable shot. The tee was moved back to the right and little ridges were dug into the fairway to halt a well-placed tee shot. Miller hit a good tee shot and marched down to the fairway feeling confident as the crowd cheered. He thought about the green coat once again and decided to go for the green on his second shot. He had a good lie and decided to use a 4-wood. Landing the ball onto the green, it then trickled all the way down to the edge of the water. He was able to make a decent chip, but missed his 10-foot birdie putt. Satisfied that he got away with a par five, Miller thought of how impossible Sarazen's double eagle had been. He then marched onto the 16th tee feeling emboldened by his now two-stroke lead and that powerful vision of him wearing the green jacket. He was going to win!

Miller bogeyed two of his last three holes and lost the green jacket to Charles Coody, who was burning up the course behind Miller. It was Charles Coody's only major and Coody would never win another PGA Tour event. Despite his vivid vision, Johnny Miller never won a green jacket.

My visions of playing golf continued but as we know, visions don't always come true.

CHAPTER TWO

In The Rough

Fantasizing about playing golf at the Royal Durban Golf Club remained just that, a fantasy. We were soon to embark on a whole other lifestyle that would only deepen my desire to play golf.

Dad was in real estate and had achieved a certain amount of success. When a property came up for sale, he decided it was land he had to have for himself. The land was several thousand acres and it was known as Blood River, the site of one of South Africa's bloodiest historical battles.

The Battle of Blood River was the name given for the battle fought between 470 Voortrekkers (Afrikaaners) led by Andries Pretorius, and an estimated 10,000–15,000 Zulus led by King of the Zulus, Dingane, on the bank of the Ncome River on December 16, 1838, in what is today known as KwaZulu-Natal, South Africa. Casualties amounted to three thousand of King Dingane's warriors, including two Zulu princes competing for the Zulu throne. Only three Voortrekkers were slightly wounded, including Pretorius himself.

In the sequel to the Battle of Blood River in January 1840, a prince named Mpande defeated Dingane and was subsequently crowned as new King of the Zulus – with the help of Mpande's new alliance partner Andries Pretorius.

Out there on Blood River, I sensed (or imagined) the spirits of the fallen Zulus. It was a haunted landscape from north to south and east to west. I heard voices and sounds when there was no one there. The land was sacred and it seemed to me that it didn't want intruders living upon it, particularly white intruders. Though we were of English descent and rejected apartheid, we were still white people whose ancestors had colonized South Africa.

My brother Tay, sister Belle, and I became aware we were moving to Blood River the night before the move. We had visited Blood River once, but we had also visited dozens of properties because Dad was in real estate. Our actually moving out into the "bush" was not something we realized was going to occur until we saw our parents packing up the Durban apartment the night before.

It wasn't that unusual – us moving without warning. We had moved a lot. Dad was never content to stay in one place for long and we always picked up and left on a moment's notice.

The next day I looked with sadness and longing at Durban as we sat in congested traffic on the highway that would take us far into the bush to Blood River. How would I ever play golf stuck out there in the bush? I wondered.

Our parents had fallen in love with American culture and months earlier had purchased a VW truck – the entire body of which was custom painted with an American flag. We three kids sat on the back of the truck cramped against luggage and boxes. Any belongings that could not fit on the truck were thrown away or abandoned. Because we had moved so frequently, our belongings were sparse to begin with.

As soon as we hit the open highway, Tay and Belle immediately began to fight in the back of the truck. Belle was in a particularly dark mood, upset about leaving the excitement of Durban's city life. I sat there in sheer misery, jostling about in the back of the truck between two bickering siblings as Dad drove at a high speed, overtook cars on blind curves, drove up on sidewalks to bypass traffic and had no hesitation about plowing through someone's yard to keep moving. Mom sat next to him, her hand gripping the back of the truck bench.

The landscape changed dramatically from dark green to pale yellow. I dreaded what awaited us out in the bush as with each mile, the scenery seemed more remote, bleak, brown and barren.

We stopped for refreshment in the small town of Dundee situated about halfway between Johannesburg and Durban. Nestled in the valley of the picturesque Biggarsberg Mountain range, Dundee languished along with a host of other small sleepy towns; all of which have a fascinating history. A number of quaint old homes and farms dotted the landscape. The region was also home to a number of skilled crafts people. Pottery, woodwork, hand knotted carpets, woven grass baskets, Zulu beadwork, were produced there for purchase. Mining of coal was being overtaken by agriculture and there were numerous cattle farms. It was a region of hot, sunny days with refreshing afternoon thunderstorms in the summer and in the winter, warm days and chilly nights perfect for a braai (a barbecue). Of interest to me was a sign marked "golf club" but I did not see the course nor did I dare ask to see it.

It was at this pit-stop in Dundee when our parents informed us that we were all going to be attending boarding school in the little town. It was just more bad news as far as we were concerned. We all had this notion that living out in the bush meant no school. Belle was suffering the most. She was into fashion and make-up and there was not much need for that living in the bush.

Fueled by this irritating news, we sulked on the back of the truck as we headed deeper into the bush toward Blood River, approximately 32 miles northeast of Dundee. Gone were the paved roads and from there on it was dirt road driving. We were bumping up and down on the back of the truck, lifting up completely off the truck bed with our heads bashing against the glass window as Dad drove at a high speed. Tay and Belle banged into each other and screamed back and forth, "Don't touch me!"

Before long, Tay and Belle were engaged in a tumbling fight. Dad pounded his fist against the back window and shook a threatening finger at them, but the fight did not abate. Soon, the truck came to a screeching halt and out stormed Dad, his fists ready to settle the matter. He flung open the truck gate, hopped up and began smacking the two of them around. I wormed my way off the truck bed and looked around at the barren land. *We were moving to this? Ugh.* I was forlorn – there was not one hint of the beautiful emerald glow that makes up fairways and greens.

After silencing his two older children with his fists, Dad continued the drive to Blood River, bumping wildly along the road which was more like a severely eroded ravine. When the truck came to a hurtling stop, we three kids all stood up in the back of the truck and eagerly looked around with anticipation. Tay and Belle still had tear-stained faces from crying over their beating. We gazed from end to end. The landscape had a raw wild beauty. We didn't see a house. We didn't see any structure. As our parents exited the cab, Dad informed us we would be living in a tent – a tent they had yet to purchase. Now this sounded like an adventure to me – a scary adventure, but Belle began to sob loudly. Tay leaped off the back of the truck to the dry ground and was screeching with laughter at Belle's appearance. Her long wavy blonde hair was knotted like a tumbleweed, her stunning green eyes were bloodshot in a dirt-covered face and little black bugs dotted her teeth. Tay's face was completely covered in dirt; his dark hair thick with the red-brown soil of Blood River. I didn't look much better.

Belle and I slowly climbed off the back of the truck into knee-high dry grass. Belle had on platform high heels while I had on flip flops. Neither of us made it very far before we were back sitting on the truck. The metal truck bed was as hot as an oven under the blazing African sun. We tried to keep our skin off it, but it was difficult to do so as we were both wearing shorts.

Dad said he had plans to develop the land into a town. Over there, he pointed, he would build houses and cottages. There, to the north, he would build tennis courts and over to the south, he would build a lake. Then, he said the magic words: "And over there, I am going to build a golf course."

I nearly fell off the back of the truck. I was shocked, elated and surprised. My own father who derided golf was going to build a golf course? We would own a golf course? That was the best news I had ever heard in my life!

I was still on cloud nine when our parents took off for Dundee to buy the tent. I walked around Blood River. The sharp dry grass cut at my feet and ankles. I didn't care. I would have my own golf course and that was the most unbelievable feeling I had experienced in my short life. I was finally going to play golf.

The sun was now low in the sky and the grassland was burnished gold. The wind picked up and the long dry grass seemed to be whispering in conspiratorial tones. I began to feel isolated and alone as those whispers grew louder in their foreign tongue.

Belle sulked for a while, found a towel amongst our luggage and used it to lie down on a bare patch of ground where she began reading a fashion magazine. Tay disappeared. He said he had to "see a man about a horse."

I tramped over to a hard pan area, found a decent stick and began to hit rocks as far as I could. I was beyond excited. I was going to fine-tune my hitting right here on Blood River while *my* golf course was being built. I hit rocks until my arms ached.

When darkness enveloped the land, the three of us huddled together. The night was crisp as we shivered in our tank tops and shorts. In the darkness, the African sky appears vast and the lack of light pollution allows one to ponder a countless array of stars but the bush remains dark, the blackest black, while strange noises and echoes emanate from the ravines, gullies and gorges.

Tay insisted that our parents would never return. I began to cry. I hugged my knees and began to rock back and forth. I bit down on my kneecap, trying to control myself from screaming with fear. Tay laughed, warning me that the bogeyman was coming for me. Belle ignored the both of us. She rolled up in a ball and tried to sleep only rousing to yell at me to stop being a big baby. I was nine, Tay was twelve and Belle was fourteen.

Finally, in the dark black night we were relieved to see two points of light as the VW truck made its way back to us. Feeling relieved at not having been abandoned or attacked by the bogeyman, uncontrollable sobbing escaped from me when they arrived. Mom reached out to me and pain coursed through my arm.

I spent the night on the back of the truck under that big African sky sandwiched between Belle and Tay while our parents slept in the cab. I didn't sleep a wink. I couldn't feel fear because I was too busy thinking about the fact that I would be playing golf very soon.

CHAPTER THREE

Hardpan

The tent was a bright tarp blue and approximately six hundred square feet. It was unwieldy and difficult to erect the next morning, particularly because we were doing so in high winds. Rather than wait for the wind to die down Dad plowed ahead, Mom shrieking with glee at the challenge of battling nature. Dad yelled at Tay to tie down one section of the tarp but my skinny brother couldn't contain it in the gale and it blew up, billowing like a giant blue parachute. Stalking over to Tay, Dad picked up the mallet and whacked Tay across the face with it. Tay grabbed his cheek and staggered to the ground.

"You useless shit!" Dad yelled.

Mom ran over to help Dad tie down that section and Belle and I did our utmost to hold down the tent until the stakes were in place, fearing Dad's wrath if we didn't. Tay got back up and silently, dutifully held down another part of the tent with his entire body. I felt horrible for him; pity and sadness. It took weeks for his bruised cheek to fully heal.

Once the tent was erected, it provided shelter from rainfall but inside, under the heat, it was stifling. The three of us spent most of our time outside, getting scorched red in the African sun. I hit rocks and drew up a golf course design modeled after the course in Durban. Belle worked on her tan and Tay went down into the gorge and painted hieroglyphics on the rock walls. He had a notion that he could bring an anthropology or archaeological team to Blood River to study "early" rock paintings so he could secretly laugh in his sleeve at them.

Our toilet consisted of walking a considerable distance from the tent and digging a hole in the ground. Our parents had plans to install a septic tank, but it was not a priority early on. If we had to go, we tried to hold it because nightfall brought out adders, large snakes – hundreds of them – that lay out in the moonlight like thick coiled ropes.

Over the next few weeks, progress on the housing development and more importantly the golf course was non-existent as Mom and Dad focused on designing one house. We still did not have plumbing. Bathing consisted of using a bucket of water, which made Belle hysterical over her inability to maintain her fluffy Farrah Fawcett hairstyle. We had been drinking bottled beverages or water that was brought in a big plastic tank, so when Dad found a well, we were grateful to finally have running water.

Our presence was becoming known to the Zulus and the white neighbors that lived in the region. One day a neighbor drove right up to our tent in his Land Rover. Dad went outside and they shook hands but after a few minutes Dad was yelling at the man and the stranger rapidly jumped into his vehicle and drove off, leaving a cloud of dust in his wake.

The man lived a few miles away and said he had tested the well water and found it contained arsenic. The man wanted to warn Dad. Dad said the man was just trying to create trouble and that there was nothing wrong with the water. It tasted just fine. However, from then on, Mom used cheesecloth to "strain" the water we drank.

Mom and Dad were having a ball designing their new house but they often went into Dundee to spend the night at the town's finest hotel so they could take a break from camping. The three of us kids remained on Blood

River in the tent using sleeping bags on top of plywood. One night two Zulus approached the tent looking for something to steal – or worse. We cowered and whimpered in the tent, but soon fearful rage overtook Tay. He grabbed his cricket bat and ran out screaming like a madman wielding the bat until the offenders ran off. It was not the last time he had to do that. Intruders would make frequent appearances. They were watching the property and struck most often when our parents were gone. Those nights our parents stayed at the hotel, none of us slept. We were too terrified to close our eyes.

To distract myself, I would think about the golf course; what it would look like. I imagined that once it was built, I would spend my days out there. I would refine my skills and be the best golfer in the world. Maybe we could even play golf as a family.

A Chicago-area veteran golfer and President of the Belmont Golf Club named Herbert J. Tweedie had done just that – enlisted his entire family into the game of golf. It was a masterstroke. Every member of the Tweedie household with the exception of the baby (who was 15 months old) played the game. Mrs. Tweedie had taken up the sport and that made for a very pleasant marriage as far as Mr. Tweedie was concerned. Violet, the oldest, won a trophy at Belmont. Doug, the oldest boy, developed the prowess of a Findlay Douglas (a Scottish amateur golfer champion who later became President of the USGA).

When the local paper interviewed the golfing Tweedies, young Doug felt he was good enough to declare to the reporter, "Dad's off his game."

Herbert's own father was one of the best amateur golfers around and had inspired his son. With his five children and wife golfing, Herbert J. Tweedie was a happy man. He was of the opinion that golf brought families together.

I dreamed that my family would have fun golfing together on Blood River. That one day Tay would swing a golf club to have fun instead of an old cricket bat to defend our lives.

*

One morning, after spending a few nights at the hotel in Dundee, we saw our parents returning to Blood River. The VW truck was coming down the road followed by a sports car, a Jaguar. Dad had bought himself a new car. Soon after, he bought Mom a brand-new Mercedes and all three vehicles sat outside our dilapidated tent. The new event in the lives of us kids, however, was not the new vehicles. It was the fact that we were about to start boarding school.

When the school term started, Belle and Tay were eager to move to Dundee so at least they would have a bed, shelter, plumbing and friends. I wanted to stay out in the bush. I wanted the solitude and I wanted to hit rocks while I watched Dad build the golf course. But we were destined for boarding school. Belle and Tay were enrolled in the high school while I went to the middle/primary school.

Belle adapted quickly. She made a lot friends and enjoyed being in town. Tay found a group of kids considered outsiders and he soon became the leader of the bunch. I spent most of my time watching the rugby matches after school.

Like the school in Durban, this school also didn't have a golf program. The merits of golf were still being debated amongst school principals. One vocal headmaster of a public school said that golf was not a good game because it ruined the temperament. Golf, he further proclaimed, failed to teach cooperation and mutual dependence on others. Not so, others argued. Golf teaches self-reliance. But that argument did not impress the vocal headmaster. He thought self-reliance was a weak feature of golf because it had a tendency to make a golfer "reserved and old before his time." Golf, the headmaster sniffed, was "a very aging game."

Though I didn't know anyone personally who played golf that did not keep me from expressing my desire to play golf to my Phys Ed teacher. Without a golf program, however, I decided to take up tennis, but it did little to replace my desire to play golf. What I didn't realize at the time was that participation in other sports actually helped prepare me for golf. From hand-to-eye coordination to visualization, focus and precision, tennis helped me make contact with a ball. Outdoor sports, however, were not the only extracurricular activities that benefited a golf game.

Wilson P. Foss was an amateur champion billiard player. He had attained a degree of skill in the game rarely attained by amateurs and was extremely fond of it. But as much as Foss liked billiards, he liked golf even more. More than one good amateur billiard player had found the allure of the links more seductive than the crack of a billiard ball and more than one good amateur billiard player had discovered his precision and skill on the table helped his golf game.

Having played both sports, Foss believed there were some similarities in golf and billiards. He thought his billiards experience had helped him a lot when it came to golf, but that golf was of no help in playing billiards. Therefore, golf was indebted to billiards as far as Foss was concerned.

For Foss, the aspect of golf that was like billiards was the putting. The practiced eye and wrist that were acquired at the billiard table helped him out on the putting green.

"In putting," Foss said, "what you need most of all is judgment of force and speed and this same quality is indispensable in playing billiards well. The control over the wrist and other parts of the arm that comes from long experience comes in handy in gauging the force and speed necessary to drive a golf ball into the hole. I think every billiard player who has taken to golf has found this to be the case."

In comparing the two games, Foss said there was one thing to be said in favor of billiards: It was by far the more scientific game of the two and a much harder game to master than golf.

"In golf there are two or three hundred players good enough to play in a tournament for first honors and fifty or sixty good enough to have a reasonable chance to win. Yet, how many are there who are good enough to have an equal chance in billiards? Of all the billiard players in the world today, there are only a handful of players that are first class. For example, one year at an amateur golf championship a young man who had finished dead last in the qualifying round went on to win. There is no such element of chance in winning a billiard tournament. The player who is behind in billiards has less chance to catch up than in golf, but the better billiard player is more likely to win."

Walter Travis was the most successful amateur golfer in the United States during the early 1900s. He later became a golf journalist and publisher, an innovative instructor in the game and a well-respected golf course architect. Foss said that if he gave Travis one-half a game of billiards he could still beat him. He doubted Travis could do the same to him in golf (though overall he knew Travis could kick his butt in a hundred straight contests at golf).

Walter Travis began to play golf at the age of 34 after being encouraged by his friends to join a new golf club they were creating. Within a month of hitting his first golf shot, Travis won the Oakland Golf Club handicap competition. Within a year, he won the Oakland Golf Club championship with a score of 82. In the time Travis reached the top, no such progress could have been made in billiards, according to Foss. The only comparison Foss could make to Travis' rise in the game of golf was the equally rapid rise of Frank Ives, who became known as the "Napoleon of Billiards."

With regard to the notion that golf required more visualization and skill than billiards, Foss cited a feat that Travis was able to accomplish. The feat consisted of Travis hitting a golf ball straight up over a seventy-five foot high tree and landing the ball onto a green ten feet from the tree. Such a shot in golf might be called phenomenal, but shots just as surprising and even more astonishing are made in billiards.

"In both games, a common mistake on the part of the player is trying to do too much and not keeping within one's ability," Foss said. "It is better to know what you can do and try to do it than trying things that are beyond you. In both games, the player finds the implements with which he is to accomplish the result while at rest. When it comes his turn to play, all he has to do is get up there and do it. Nothing depends on his opponent - everything depends on himself."

Foss said if he had to give up one game for the other, he would give up billiards without a moment's hesitation. Though he found both golf and billiards to be great recreation, the sensation of driving a golf ball and having

it land right where he figured it would was a joy he never
experienced in billiards.

Not being able to play golf or billiards, I immersed
myself in tennis. But I still looked upon it as a poor
substitute for golf.

At my boarding school, the principal was high profile.
He would walk around campus and talk to pupils. He
would often ask, "What do you want to be when you
grow up?"

I was extremely introverted and very obedient to
authority figures. The day the principal approached me
with that question, I stammered, "I... I want to play
golf."

The principal hitched up his pants and frowned at
me. "You know that is a men's sport, don't you?"

"I... well, I..."

"You're a girl."

I lowered my head. "Yes."

"Only unpleasant women with thick ankles want to
play golf. Do you have thick ankles?"

I looked down at my skinny ankles. "No sir."

The boys who were eavesdropping on the
conversation were laughing at me as the principal left to
talk to another student.

"Dyke!" one of the boys yelled.

I didn't know why the boy was calling me a dam or a
levee, but it wasn't pleasant. I didn't know that was a
derogatory term for a lesbian until one of the girls in the
dorm told me. I knew I wasn't a lesbian and yet I loved
golf. It was all very confusing.

*

On weekends, it was back to Blood River.
Construction was moving fast on our house as Dad had
hired four local Zulus to help build it. He paid them well
but he treated them horribly with physical abuse

whenever they did something wrong. They had never done any residential construction before so therefore made many mistakes, yet Dad expected them to be expert laborers.

Our parents designed our house to be a replica of a wagon akin to the wagons the Voortrekkers had used coming across the African plain. My parents did not like Afrikaners very much because of apartheid so I wasn't sure why they were building something that was reminiscent of the Boer-Zulu war.

Our house had four giant wheels, a massive arched corrugated iron roof to mimic a covered wagon and the walkway in front of the house had a hitching ramp. Visitors seeking out Blood River's official monument a few miles down the road would mistakenly stop by our house thinking that it was the monument.

We three kids were excited at the thought of once again living under a roof with plumbing when we came home from boarding school, but we were wrong. The three of us continued to live in the tent while our parents lived in the new four-bedroom, two-bath house. Fortunately, we spent the week in boarding school so we did not have to live in the tent except on weekends and holidays. Most of the wildlife had moved far enough away from the tent, but we always had to watch for the poisonous snakes that would slip under the tarp. Tay became an expert at chopping the head off of invading snakes with a shovel. We just had to wait until morning to use the bathroom in the wagon house because Dad was tired of running into our "land mines" out in the scrub.

One weekend Tay brought home a friend named Billy. He was an "orphan" – a kid who lived at boarding school year round because he did not have parents. Tay thought inviting him back to Blood River would be fun for both of them.

Billy was quiet and reserved, pale, short and wiry, with a huge mop of dark hair. He and Tay spent most of the weekend running around outdoors, laughing and joking and making mud pies. On Saturday night, the boys were to take turns taking a bath in the wagon house. There was no shower installed so a bath was the only option.

Billy took his bath first. He emerged out of the bathroom with state-issued pajamas and bare feet, his thick hair sopping wet. Tay laughed at him and the two needled each other for a while in the living room as I sat in the corner and used crayons to color in my golf course design.

I heard Dad's feet thumping along the floor as he made his way to us. He grabbed Billy by his wet hair and started smacking our guest around.

Tay began shrieking, "No!"

Dad kept hitting Billy. "You think you can come into my house and leave a dirty bath tub? You think my wife is your kaffir?" (Kaffir is a derogatory term for a black person).

Billy cowered on the carpet, crawling into a ball. I kept my head down as much as possible, my tears saturating my golf course drawing. I was afraid of Dad, but Tay was different. He wasn't cowering or crying like he used to. He glared at Dad; his entire being seething with hatred. Dad had crossed a line and so had Tay. There was no going back for either one of them.

Billy spent the rest of the weekend in the tent never emerging to eat or to use the bathroom. Early Monday morning, he rode on the back of the VW truck with Tay as Dad drove us back to boarding school. We never saw Billy again and we never invited another friend home.

*

I never stopped hitting rocks and waiting for my father to build the golf course. Each weekend, I would come home from boarding school, hoping to find the golf course built or at least started, but I was always disappointed. I was frustrated at the non-start, staring at my father, trying to bore my eyes into him so I could will him into starting construction.

The South African plain is called the bushveld and is dotted by dense clusters of trees and tall shrubs. The grass is yellow or brown and tall. Much of it towered over my head. It was difficult flora in which to hit rocks and it covered every square inch of Blood River so I did not have many options unless I played out in the dirt road, but then Dad would yell, "Get out of the bloody road!" which was probably a good thing given how reckless a driver he was.

In the bushveld there is a constant smell of dry grass and other scents emanating from the earth – the soil and the animal droppings. The bushveld is always alive; moving and swaying, rustling and speaking in whispers. Its voice is drowned out only by the orchestra of crickets and cicada.

Trying to play golf in the bushveld was not easy but it was not necessarily an unusual setting. Finding a way to play golf wherever you are seems to be something lovers of the game just do. Back in the 1930s, employees of Pan-Am Airways who worked the trans-Pacific route made Midway Island their golf destination.

About 1,380 miles west of Hawaii, Midway Island rises approximately 50 feet above sea level. Covered with fine white sand and a thick tangle of scrub, the Pan-Am crew set up nine golf holes along the beach. The crew marked the holes with poles tied with rags. They named the "course" "Goofey Gooney Gulf" or "Gooneyville" after the large number of birds blanketing the island known as goonies. The golf balls were painted red to distinguish them from the white gooney eggs that were laid all over the island. The crew often played golf shirtless, in swim trunks with a pair of sneakers to keep their feet off the hot sand. With thousands of goonies squawking around them, it was not a quiet afternoon on the beach links. The birds didn't budge out of the "fairway" and threw tantrums when a ball landed on or near them. For putting, the players first measured where their ball was from the "flag" and then smoothed out a path. The goonies didn't care about the etiquette of being quiet when the players attempted their putts.

I had not set up any flag pins or even tried my hand at putting and the most treacherous hazard for me was trying to avoid poisonous snakes. I did all of my hitting barefoot because I could not get enough rotation and stability wearing flip flops but in truth, my swing was an undisciplined sweeping motion. I also did not set up specific targets to hit to because I simply did not have enough knowledge of the game. My bare feet were calloused walking over all that spiky grass and sharp rocks, but it allowed me to feel stable when I took a swing. I felt limited and awkward when I wore shoes.

Sam Snead learned to play golf barefoot and actually preferred it, not just because of the sensation of the cool grass beneath his warm toes. He felt a connection to the earth in his stance that prevented him from over-swinging. He said by practicing barefoot, he learned to swing the club nice and easy. When he did play with shoes on, he felt like he had two bricks on his feet and he was not able to execute the shots as he desired. Wearing shoes went against what he believed was an essential ingredient to a nice and easy swing. Shoes made playing more difficult, sent tension through his neck and arms and caused him to miss short putts, something he feared, he said, as much as getting struck by lightning on the course (he grew up in an area where lightning strikes were frequent).

Snead thought it was ridiculous that he was required to wear shoes. Since he was a child, he had been practicing barefoot even though rattlesnakes waited for him like landmines. He was passionate about the game and went through his homemade wood clubs so frequently he would have to whittle a new one every few days.

Only Old Man Winter put shoes on Snead's feet but by then he had no toenails left and his feet had become leathery and calloused, so it was not as if he was feeling much anyway. He only wore shoes to avoid frostbite.

Snead played golf barefoot until he reached high school and then he acquired a bag of used clubs. He tried to make his own golf shoes by hammering some spikes into his street shoes, but it took away all the feel and rhythm of his swing. For the first time, he was feeling like golf was complicated. This was when Snead became aware of how thinking too much about his feet or his stance or his swing or anything else negatively impacted his game. He believed in relying upon natural imagination; see the shot, telegraph how you wanted to execute the shot to your muscles and fire away rather than have the thought, "How does my swing look?" He thought too many golfers were trying to "pose" to impress their friends with the technicalities of their swing rather than swing in a natural way.

Snead felt shoes were an impediment to his natural swing and that is why he wanted to play barefoot, but the etiquette of golf forbade him from doing so.

Snead did get an opportunity to play barefoot as a professional and he relished the opportunity to take those bricks off his feet and let loose. It was at the 1937

Open Championship in Carnoustie, Scotland. Snead hit a shot right into the water. He made his way over to his ball and gleefully flung off his shoes. He got down in the cool water, enjoying the way it refreshed his feet and he blasted it out of there onto the green to make par. He had to put his shoes back on for the rest of the tournament, but getting to take off his shoes was one of his favorite memories of that event.

At another tournament in Miami one year, Snead's ball buried in mud. Again, he gleefully took off his shoes and got his feet into the muck. He swung at the ball. Mud went flying into his mouth and eye, but out of his other eye he witnessed his ball bounce onto the green. The mud ball hopped and meandered before landing smack dab into the hole. Snead believed it was because of his bare feet.

At a practice round at the Masters, Snead did get a chance to play golf barefoot. He was criticized severely as making a mockery of the sport and that it was grossly undignified. Many who came to watch him practice remarked that it was not possible to play barefoot, but Snead played two holes barefoot and birdied them both. Due to the uproar, he put his shoes back on to appease the critics but also for another reason He had been playing tournament golf in shoes for so long his bare feet were aching.

Snead laughed that the game was considered a fine gentleman's sport because he really saw it as a country kid's game.

And for me it was a country kid's game – even in the bush in South Africa.

Every weekend for two years I hit rocks barefoot on Blood River until the circumstances of life made me put the shoes back on my feet.

CHAPTER FOUR

Unstable Lie

South Africa was changing. Apartheid was untenable and unacceptable for the majority in the country and riots began breaking out everywhere protesting the government's segregation law. Living in South Africa was becoming a frightening, unsettling and deeply traumatic reality but it was not only black versus white conflict and turmoil that was occurring. With several different tribes living in South Africa, each tribe wanted to position themselves to ultimately become the leading tribe of the country. No one knew how things would turn out, but many feared an apocalypse, including myself. I became a bundle of nerves based on the riots, anger, violence and upheaval all around me. It was unsafe to be on the streets, but it also felt unsafe to be at home.

News was very difficult to come by. The South African government worked full-time on censorship of anything it deemed inappropriate, whether it was music, pop culture or news. Censorship, however, could not prevent us from seeing that the country was spiraling out of control.

Intruders were increasingly coming to our house on Blood River to steal property or confront my father. On those nights when our parents left us alone to stay at the hotel in Dundee (they still did that even though they had the house), Tay, now age fourteen, took up his cricket bat and defended us with a maniacal look in his eye. My brother had changed dramatically in the last two years. He had gone from a thin kid to a muscular brute and he frequently expressed his desire to have his cricket bat make contact with a thief's head.

I slept very little on Blood River, petrified at every sound while Tay sat, watchful, waiting, itching to hurt anyone who entered our tent.

There is a song by Buffalo Springfield called *For What It's Worth* that contains the following lines:

Paranoia strikes deep
Into your life it will creep
It starts when you're always afraid

That is what had happened to Tay and it was also happening to me. I had no idea how deep the seed of paranoia had been planted in me and how it would manifest in the years to come.

One dark night on Blood River there was banging against our tent, loud noises and shouting in Zulu. I quickly sat up in my sleeping bag and hugged my knees to my chest and began shaking and crying. I was petrified. Belle hid under the cover of her sleeping bag. Tay got up and lit a kerosene lamp. It illuminated a malevolent leer on his face as he grabbed his cricket bat. He burst out of the tent, swinging. A large spotlight fell on him. He stopped in his tracks. I heard a roar of laughter and I slowly crept over to peer outside the tent. Tay was standing there with the bat hanging limply beside him. There were no intruders. Our parents had crept back in the night and were pretending to be marauders as a joke.

In my fear I had peed my pants. If Mom and Dad found out about it, I would be in big trouble. I quickly hurried back to my sleeping bag to hide under the wet covers. No one ever found out and my sleeping bag was never washed.

I felt better staying at boarding school. I was able to rest there in the early evening because I shared a dorm room with 11 other girls. As soon as the lights went out, however, the girls were quiet and it was dark, so very dark. Every sound sent a little shock through me. I was wide-eyed, afraid and sleepless. When I was able to get a grip on myself, I would dissipate my fear by thinking about playing golf on Blood River. Those thoughts were the only distraction that took me outside of that bubble of fear. It was a comfort and I was able to fall asleep. I didn't know at the time that the dream of playing golf on Blood River was rapidly slipping away from me.

One late Friday afternoon, my parents arrived to pick me up from boarding school. I thought it was going to be a typical weekend on Blood River, but they informed me that it was my last day in Dundee because we were moving back to the city of Durban. As I quickly threw my belongings in a box, I was in a state of shock for a number of reasons. It was the middle of the school year, I never said goodbye to my boyfriend, my friends or my teachers and I also realized that my dream of a golf course on Blood River was gone forever. Dad had built the house, the lake, one tennis court and one extra cottage, but he never broke ground on the golf course. When they found out, Belle and Tay were also shocked. The three of us cried all the way to Durban – in the back of the truck travelling at high speed.

*

The city had changed a lot in two years. There was more crime, protests, anger and violence. We left our apartment very little to go out except to school, the grocery store or when we felt like braving the walk to the beach. Living in fear became a way of life as people were being burned alive in the streets.

All across the world, countries were condemning South Africa with the belief that every single white person was racist. It simply was not true; not for me and not for many other whites. We rejected apartheid just as most of the world did. For South Africans, how society would integrate – given the many different ethnicities - was the biggest concern, but the world continued to believe it was a black versus white issue.

One bright representative of South Africa, the emblem shining out there always to give some counter to all the (understandable) bad press about South Africa was Gary Player. He also thought apartheid was unjust but he often spoke of good things in the country, like the phenomenal beauty and fascinating variety of culture.

Player's small stature evaporated under the largeness of his game. He talked tough, was didactic but he also was magnanimous and one hell of a player. Never more fitting was a surname than Player. Despite traveling the world, he always came back to South Africa when he could have easily settled in the United States. Doing that would have been easier on his life and family, but instead, he stayed true to his country and in doing so, South Africa shined along with him during a bleak and shameful time.

At the age of 29, Player won the 1965 U.S. Open becoming the only non-American to win all four majors (the career Grand Slam). He went on to accumulate 165 professional wins, tied with Sam Snead. Jack Nicklaus has 115 professional wins. Arnold Palmer has 95 professional wins.

When Player won his first Masters in 1961, he was portrayed in the media as full of himself, and when it was reported that he had confided to a friend, "The Lord wants me to win" many felt he was an arrogant weirdo.

That day in April, Player could never have imagined how it would unfold. At first, he could do no wrong. Trees offered assistance on his approaches. An over-clubbed shot became a birdie when a spectator deflected the ball. And when he was losing his last round lead, a massive storm halted play.

At the resumption of play, the Golf God began to toy with Player. On the final back nine, nothing seemed to go right – like when a shot on the par 5 13th hole landed on a twig, it took him seven strokes to get down. Player walked off the 18th green close to tears and one stroke behind *the* man, defending champion Arnold Palmer, who needed only a par on 18 to win.

As Player watched from the clubhouse, Palmer bladed a sand shot over the green and double bogeyed the hole. Player, shocked and then elated, had captured his first green jacket.

The American media, in particular, did not warm to him at first and called Player "flamboyant" and "offbeat" indicating that in a game dominated by robot-like young men prone to silence and conservative dress, Gary Player was a bit of a heretic. His living habits were scrutinized and deemed eccentric. "He neither smokes nor drinks," sniffed one media outlet. "He subsists on bizarre dishes like scallops and honey, orange juice, wheat germ, nuts and raisins."

"I guess that's all right," Palmer said, when asked what he thought of Player's diet, "…if you like nuts and raisins."

Player was the most animated golfer to join the pro golf tour since Water Hagen and Jim Demaret. Like them, Player believed in hamming it up for the galleries. Conservative officials winced when he said, "Tournament golf has to be something of a show for the spectators." To make his point, one year he showed up at St. Andrews wearing pants with one white leg and one black leg. "They were a bit stuffy about it," Player said. "And two ladies even got into a row about it. I had to change."

The year Player won his first Masters, he was wearing all black. The media demanded to know why. "Black gives me strength," Player said. Player's nickname ultimately became The Black Knight.

The press mocked his rather mystical response and continued to portray him as a bit of an outsider, but ultimately, he would become one of the great ambassadors of the game and Gary Player remains a South African hero not only for the way he played golf but how he was able to bring a ray of light to South Africa during a particularly dark period.

I had taken on a lot of feelings of shame and embarrassment about South Africa's apartheid policy and I think that Gary Player did as much or more than the other anti-apartheid fighters in a dignified and fair-minded manner. Sports have a way of transcending differences. South African golf, along with rugby, was one of our few saving graces.

Long before Gary Player made it to the US Tour there was another South African who took America by storm. When South African Bobby Locke arrived in the United States on April Fool's Day of 1947, he began a torrid run. He won seven tournaments by August of that year thus becoming the leading money winner.

Locke amused the gallery with his baggy knickers and floppy cap, the ease and naturalness with which he conducted himself and the way he bent his left arm on his back swing. Somehow with that swing he was tremendously accurate off the tee and from the fairway. Some opined he hit so many fairways and greens because he had grown up on South African courses where landing in the rough was punishing to the scorecard.

Bobby Locke is credited with the phrase, "You drive for show, but putt for dough." He was considered a genius on the greens. He could read breaks very well and he putted with an over-spin stroke. He could also intentionally hook and slice putts. Locke was a phenomenal player but two years later he found himself banned from the PGA Tour.

It was believed by some that Locke got carried away with the allure of financial reward in America because he made several commitments to appear in lucrative tournaments and exhibitions but then never showed up and gave no reason for his absence. Others claimed that his rip-roaring success angered other players and there was a conspiracy to get him off the tour. The ban was lifted in 1951, but Locke refused to return to playing in the United States, except for a few appearances. Instead, he travelled the world, accumulating 72 professional wins, including 4 Open Championships. But his final Open win in 1957 at St. Andrews was fraught with controversy. He failed to properly replace his ball after marking it on the 72nd green and proceeded to putt out. It was confirmed through newsreel footage provided to the R&A after Locke had been presented with the trophy. Locke's win could have been overturned through disqualification, but the committee decided not to disqualify him, citing "equity and spirit of the game."

Once again Bobby Locke was despised by other touring pros. Two years later, Locke was involved in a serious car accident. The injuries were debilitating and all but ended Locke's career.

Locke's astonishing number of wins raised a lot of questions. What if Locke had not been banned from the PGA Tour? What if he had returned to the tour when the ban was lifted? How many more tournaments could he have won had he not been involved in that accident? No one will ever know, but not everyone resented his success. Bobby Locke was inducted into the World Golf Hall of Fame in 1977.

Ten years later, Bobby Locke died at the age of 69 in South Africa, a year after one of the bloodiest episodes of violence in the country.

*

The increasing violence in Durban and in the country at large also included calls for the release of Nelson Mandela from prison. South Africa was becoming a bleaker more frightening place. There was blood in the streets, blood splattered on buildings and the acrid smell of burning flesh. My parents decided we had to leave the country. The problem was we didn't know where to go.

Over the next several years we traveled to several different countries, always returning to South Africa because it was required by immigration law. People in these other countries would interrogate us about apartheid, express their anger at the policy and demand to know how we could have such a law. I didn't debate the issue. I didn't say I was against apartheid. What good would it do? I was white. That was the badge that declared I was guilty. I felt attacked and berated, guilty and ashamed. I stopped speaking because I feared people would hear my South African accent. Tay faked an American accent (poorly) to avoid confrontations. Perhaps that was the just legacy due white South Africans. We deserved to suffer for what our ancestors and country had done.

When our parents finally decided to choose America and specifically Southern California as the place to live, it was a jolt to my already frazzled system. Having lived in a country with heavy censorship and racial segregation, the culture shock was jarring. The people in California were so free with their lives, their clothes and their behavior. "Laid back" it was called. I went from a rigid and regimented lifestyle to a loose lifestyle literally overnight. It was not something I embraced easily.

How could I? I had always been controlled by rules, laws, words or fists. I had no clue who I was or how to act. I even went to school wearing my South African school uniform because I had no idea that kids in America wore just about whatever they wanted to public schools.

When the male teachers learned I was from South Africa, without fail, it always led to a conversation about Gary Player that led to a wider conversation about golf. I didn't know much about golf history then, but I would listen intently as they spoke of golfers past and present: Vardon, Hogan, Ouimet, Hagen, Nelson, Park, Snead, Nicklaus and Palmer. They seemed like giants of the game – men of great accomplishment. I wanted to know more about them. I wanted to see them play. And I wanted to play just like them. But it soon became clear to me that women who golfed were not taken seriously by the men I encountered. They were either considered wannabe jocks, lesbians or uncouth. I kept my desire to play golf to myself.

In South Africa, I had a focused education that I took seriously. In So Cal, kids talked back to their teachers, ditched school to go to the beach and wore clothes tighter than I had ever seen. High school was a social gathering rather than a place to learn. That rattled me. Tay and Belle assimilated much better, relishing the freedom.

One of the great things about where we were renting a house in Southern California was the proximity to a well-stocked library. This is where I spent the majority of my time those first few years of living in America. I felt safe in that space. I did not have to talk to anyone and I got to spend the entire time trying to find books and articles to learn more about golf.

Trying to learn how to play golf out of a book was not rare or unusual. It was how many people, including Donald Nelson, chairman of the War Production Board during World War II, learned the game. He picked up Alex Morrison's *A New Way To Better Golf* and was so able to grasp the game, particularly off the tee, that he outdrove pro golfer Sam Snead at a driving contest.

I culled every inch of the local library looking for instruction books and articles about golf. When I stumbled upon a stack of old *Golf Illustrated* magazines I was stoked. Unfortunately, many of the pages were missing or torn or ruined, but I was still able to read enough of the magazine to enjoy some of the articles.

One article covered the first and second rounds between Englishman Harry Vardon and Willie Park Jr. of Scotland in a match at North Berwick, East Lothian (Scotland). It essentially was the first golf match that I became aware of since we did not have television in South Africa and I had never seen an entire round of golf played before.

The match wasn't especially dramatic or of great significance, but the article was important to me because I was able to visualize how a round of golf is played based on the writer's vivid description of the match. Until this account, I didn't know there were undulating fairways that made for tough lies or how difficult it was to chip from around the green or the hazards of landing in a bunker. This match gave me valuable insight. It would become a treasured keepsake that I had just about committed to memory:

> Of the two men, Vardon was the better known to the majority of the public, certainly to the majority of English ones. Except for his annual appearance in the Open Championships, Park was

comparatively little known outside of Scotland though Park himself was a two-time Open Champion and the son of an Open Champion. This was a distinction that had only so far been attained by one other golfing family, namely, the Morrises (Tom Sr. and Tom Jr.) of St. Andrews.

Willie Park Jr. could further boast the unique distinction of having had a Champion uncle, Mungo Park of Scotland, who won the Open Championship in 1874. Another uncle, David Park, although he never quite succeeded in winning Championship honors, was also a good player, and in foursome-play, he and Willie Park Sr. were a formidable couple, and won many memorable matches.

Willie Park, Jr., therefore, came of grand golfing stock, and he was a worthy descendant of the men who, along with the Dunns, made Musselburgh the successful rival of St. Andrews. His golfing career thus far had been a brilliant one. He won his first Championship when he was only twenty-three years old, repeating his success two years later.

Park played a somewhat in and out game, for while he accomplished some brilliant performances and defeated some of the most formidable players, he appeared to have lost some of his form for a time. He lacked practice due to the demands of his ever-increasing golf club business. For this match, however, he had not only returned to form at the age of thirty-five, but in the opinion of competent judges, his game was now far superior to what it had ever been. His play in the Open Championship at Prestwick the prior year (1898) was a revelation, not only to many who had never seen him before, but to his old admirers. His driving was more powerful and straighter than ever before, while his approach shots and putting were absolutely masterful. His methods and style were distinct from the rest of his peers. If he appeared to lack the dash and fire of the modern school, he was captivating with his grace and skill. The ease and accuracy with which he played his half and quarter strokes was a thing to admire.

If Harry Vardon could not boast like Park of a distinguished golfing ancestry, he could at least claim to have accomplished a lot before the age of thirty.

Both players were popular. There had never been such a big crowd at a golf match, from 4,000 in the morning to about 8,000 before the match was finished. There were several ropes in use to control the gallery and to protect the greens.

The course had been shortened at various points and the tees put forward to make room for the crowd. The Committee had even asked Park himself to determine where the holes were to be placed. Park, evidently believing in his "approaching" power, had generally placed the hole near the guarding hazard so that a running approach by Vardon would not fare well.

The players shook hands cordially when they met at the first tee a few minutes before eleven o'clock. "Fiery" (Park's usual caddie) was in attendance, but a second caddie named Flynn was added, who carried an extra set of clubs. Vardon's chief club-bearer was his brother Tom, who had for an assistant the young North Berwick professional, J. L. Hutchinson. F.G. Tait acted as referee for Park at his request; and Mr. Broadwood in Vardon's case. The two refs chose as umpire Edward Blyth, one of the oldest and best North Berwick golfers. Tait was provided with two flags, one bearing the letter "P" in black and the other the letter "V" in red. There were also two sets of fore-caddies, the first looking after the balls driven from the tee; the second, taking an overlook of the approaches.

Umpire Blyth addressed some words to the gallery as to keeping order and then Park and Vardon struck off, both with their irons. They played short of the road. Vardon's second with a five iron lay nice on the green while Park scruffed his approach and just managed to reach the top of the hill, but he lay the ball six feet from the hole before holing out. Vardon took the orthodox two on the green.

The second hole, The Sea Hole, both had good drives, but Park had a bad lie and could not get his second any distance, while Vardon had to keep away to the left so as to open up the hole. Both reached the green in their third strokes and halved in five.

In driving for the third hole known as The Trap, both reached well up to the wall, and Vardon, going for the pin, fell short of the bunker. Willie kept to the left and lay short with his third, while Vardon, extricating himself neatly, had a seven foot putt for a four. Park, from the edge of the green, ran down a putt of eight yards and got a hearty cheer. Vardon did what he needed for a half in four.

To the Par 3 Carl Kemp Hole, both had excellent drives. Park was short and scarcely on the green while Vardon flew past the hole and eventually had a four yard putt to make a three. Park, again putting splendidly, got down in two.

Both were on the green at the Hole o' Cross in two, and a half in four was again called.

Fine drives found both in the Quarry in going for the sixth hole. The pitches reached the green safely, but Park had to play the odds, and the succession of halves was kept up with somewhat monotonous steadiness. It looked as if this monotony were to be broken at the Burn Hole, for while both were on the green in two, Vardon lay "stony" for four, while Park left himself with a nasty five foot putt to get the same. He went down once more amid applause.

Going to the Linkhouse Hole, Park for once outdrove his opponent. Vardon had the best of matters on the green, having laid his approach within four yards, but failed to hole. Park secured a half in five with another deadly putt.

It was only at the eleventh hole that the spell was broken, and this was partly due to a curious incident which occurred in the driving. Park's long stroke lay in a hollow, and Vardon's ball struck a ridge, rebounded on to Park's ball and knocked it about eight inches out of its position into a nasty sandy cup. When the players came up, there was a consultation between the referees as to the lifting of Park's ball and replacing it in its original position, which was done after Vardon played the odd. Had this been done at once, Park's ball would have been within six inches of Vardon's and liftable; and this should have been done, but Park's ball was allowed to lie until after Vardon played. This seemed to put off Vardon because his next two shots were duffed while his opponent was down in four. For the first time, the single flag, with the letter P, was waved, proclaiming that at last the challenger had taken the lead.

On the next hole, Vardon pulled his ball and was in rough country. He got out well, and as Park pulled his second shot, they lay near each other to the left, and the hole was halved in five.

At the tee for the Pit hole, Park took his cleek (about the equivalent of a 1-iron) for what reason no one could explain. He pulled it badly over the wall to the left, the ball being found almost unplayable. After an ineffectual stroke, he gave up the hole and the match stood all- square.

In going for the 14th Perfection hole, Vardon pulled his shot. He would have found himself in difficulties by the seashore but for the fact that the ball struck one of the spectators and was playable enough though on rough grass. With his cleek he got on the green while Park, after a fine brassie stroke, curiously hooked his shot as if to bring it around the side of the hill. The hole was halved in four.

Vardon had a beauty at the Par 3 15th Redan, his drive laying him a few yards from the hole. Park sliced his shot, which sent it into the hollow beyond the green to an impossible lie. He took four to Vardon's three and was now one down.

In going to the 16th Gate hole, both players with their second shots kept short of the dry ditch. Each ran up their shots and a half in five was called.

The match was brought level at the Par 4 17th Point Garry hole in quite a sensational manner. Both players were short of the road bunker in two.

Park, playing the odds, pulled his ball, which ran through the crowd and found a disagreeable place for itself on the rocky beach. He had to use a left-hand club and played back, just managing to get up. Then he had to play two more but he laid his long putt within six feet and holed out in six.

Vardon (who had the hole in hand) putted so timidly that he actually lost the hole in seven. His short putt was the worst of all his misses. It was no more than two feet.

At the final Par 4 Home hole, Park reached the green in two with a neat pitch, but his opponent, who had driven to the left, misjudged the line a little and his approach landed in the hollow to the left. Down in four to Vardon's five, Park thus stood one up on the first round and came in for a good deal of cheering and congratulations from his friends. Vardon shot 79 to Park's 76 in the first round.

One on-course reporter had difficulty keeping score and reported the players shot 80-80. But the day was not over. The men had to go back out again at 3:30 p.m. to start the second round. Vardon ultimately prevailed.

Finding the written account of the Vardon/Park match was the most significant advance I had made in my understanding of how golf is played. I had also found a map of the North Berwick golf course and I was able to follow the match hole by hole. Though not to scale, I would move Tic-Tacs along the map to mark each player's position – one orange for Park and one white for Vardon.

Even though the match had been played over 80 years prior and was of little historical value, it was new, fresh and important to me. I cherished that *Golf*

Illustrated piece and made photocopies of it so I could read it before bed. I would lie awake and fantasize about being one of those golfers.

It didn't matter if I was Vardon or Park. I just wanted to play golf.

CHAPTER FIVE

Fore!

The first golf club I ever touched and swung was a men's 1-iron with a stiff shaft and I couldn't make contact with the ball to save my life.

We were living in Bonsall, California, at that time a rural part of San Diego County with many horse farms. Our parents had decided to buy a house with ten acres that had a sweeping view of the valley and was isolated from other houses. It was a two-bedroom, two-bath house with a covered front porch. Mom and Dad took the master bedroom and made the spare room Dad's office. Belle slept on the covered porch while Tay slept on a pull-out bed in the living room. I slept on a cot in the kitchen pantry, a 6 x 8 room, amongst the cans of sauce and vegetables, pasta and rice.

The back door to the house was accessed through the pantry. It was a rickety aluminum door with a thin Plexi-glass window and the doorknob was right next to my head when I lay flat on the cot. One night while I was sleeping, someone rattled the doorknob trying to break into the house. I looked up and saw a man through the Plexi-glass window. I started screaming. He turned quickly and ran off, disappearing into the dark night. Dad ran into the pantry, demanding to know why I was screaming. I pointed to the door and said there was a man there.

Dad bent down, peering out the window. "There's nothing there, you stupid tit!"

Dad clobbered me and went back to bed. The image of that man trying to break in repeated in my head over and over again. I was trembling with fear. My belief that

America was a safe country and I no longer had to fear nighttime intruders was shattered.

I was afraid, but I was more afraid of my own father so whenever I heard noises in the night, even the turn of the back doorknob, I buried my head under the covers. Only when supplies and tools started disappearing from our yard did Dad believe there were thieves in the night.

Dad was selling off parcels of Blood River for cents on the rand (South African currency) to fund our lives in America. He then took the bulk of his remaining money and invested it in gold. He bought a Mercedes for Mom and a Ford truck with a double cab for himself. He also bought a used VW Rabbit for Belle so she could get a job now that she was done with high school. Within six months, Belle was living with a man twenty-five years older than her. Mom spent all her time calling his house, harassing him. He tried to be pleasant and reason with her since Belle was over 18 (barely), but Mom was relentless. One day, after she called to harass him again he called Mom "a mean bitch." She never called back again. Belle was now gone from the house, only visiting once or twice a month. I deeply envied her escape from our parents.

Tay and I continued to attend school – or at least I continued to attend school. Tay made numerous friends who had cars and he spent more time ditching school than attending it.

As they did on Blood River, our parents often left to spend a few days in a hotel by the coast and we were left alone. Because Tay was always cruising in cars with his new buddies, it meant that when our parents were gone, he wouldn't come home at all. I would be at the house by myself all night. I was thirteen years old. While I dreaded it, Tay saw it as a chance at freedom, to hang out all night.

One morning after I had spent the night alone, I heard a loud roar. I looked out the window and saw a monster truck was in our driveway. The passenger door swung open and Tay jumped down from the souped-up vehicle, his eyes bleary. He waved goodbye to his friend and came into the house with a grin on his face.

"Do you want to go play golf?" he asked me.

I thought he was joking; trying to make a fool of me so he could laugh at my frustration, but he insisted he was serious. Excitement surged through me and I leaped to my feet, ready to give it a go.

Without asking permission, Tay took Dad's keys to the Ford truck and we drove to the bottom of our driveway. Tay stopped the truck and jumped out, disappearing into the scrub. I looked after him, wondering what was going on. He then emerged out of the bushes with a set of golf clubs.

"Where'd you get those?" I asked.

"I found them."

He flung the clubs on the back of the truck and off we went.

Tay drove a few miles down to the San Luis Rey Downs Golf and Country Club in Bonsall, California. He parked on the side of the road parallel to the golf course, grabbed the clubs and casually strolled onto one of the fairways. I scurried behind him, trying to keep up. We were wearing jeans, flip flops and tank tops. Neither of us had a clue as to proper golf attire, but I doubt Tay would have cared if he was aware.

Tay gave me the 1-iron and two scuffed golf balls and then took off with the rest of the bag. I examined the balls, fascinated by the dimples. It was the first time I had held a golf ball and it meant a lot to me. I didn't even want to hit the precious thing.

In addition to the fact that I couldn't swing that men's club, I had no orientation of the course. Because we had snuck onto the course and were not allowed to be there (a fact that eluded me at the time), we were starting in the middle of some fairway. I didn't question why we were not heading for the first tee, I just followed Tay, assuming he knew what he was doing.

It was the first time I set foot on a golf course and I savored it. I felt like I was doing something worthwhile and important, but despite all my reading about golf I still had little grasp of the game. At one point I got completely turned around and was hacking from the green to the tee box. Soon enough, I lost both of my golf balls.

Tay didn't care what I was doing. He was focused on blasting his drive anywhere he felt like it. He teed it up in the middle of the fairway, aimed sideways and intentionally hit it over three fairways. He had no shame, no fear and unfortunately, no conscience. He didn't just take divots, he excavated the course.

We bounced around the empty course the entire afternoon. I truly had no concept that my brother was stealing a round of golf. I just followed him. I had never seen golf on television, so there was no clear sense of how to conduct oneself on a golf course. Playing golf with Tay, who obeyed no rules, ever, did not help with properly educating me about the game.

Finally, a gray-haired man came chasing us down in a golf cart and with a litany of expletives, told us to get lost. It was the first and last time I would be on a golf course with my brother.

That evening, Tay dropped me off at the house after buying me a meal at McDonalds. He took Dad's Ford truck to go see his friends while I went into the house to prepare for another long night alone. I turned on every single light in the house, turned up the stereo to high volume and locked myself in the bathroom. I didn't sleep a wink, watching the clock, anticipating the morning light.

The next morning, I was shocked when my parents drove up in the Mercedes with Tay in the backseat. How did they get together? They were supposed to be at the hotel and Tay was supposed to be hanging out with friends.

Tay's dark brown eyes were bloodshot, he had scratches on his face and a bruised cheek. Dad kept hitting him while Mom screamed at him. From what I could gather, Tay had crashed the blue Ford truck while travelling at a high speed. It was totaled. Dad had not taken out any insurance on the vehicle because he didn't believe in paying for insurance so there was no coverage to buy another vehicle and no coverage for the passenger (Tay's friend) who was severely injured in the crash.

Tay was beaten over the course of several hours. He was in so much pain, terrified of Dad but he never fought back or else he probably would have been killed. It was the worst most vivid day of my life watching Tay being beaten within an inch of his life. I knew that Tay was in the wrong for what he had done but I also knew my Dad was in the wrong for the corporal punishment. It was a living nightmare.

For me, the only good thing about that house in Bonsall was that it had a sweeping view of the valley. Smack dab in the middle of that view was the San Luis Rey Downs Golf Course. I was afraid to go back there because of the marshal, but my parents also continued to strongly discourage me from pursuing golf. They sternly impressed upon me that nothing – nothing – was worth pursuing unless I was making money at it. They saw golf as a folly, not as a serious endeavor – a way to make real money.

Pro golfer Billy Casper once said there were two ways to play golf, for money and for fun. Anyone can do both but for him it was a job and going to the course was like going to the office, except his office was outside in the sunshine (usually).

He appreciated his life as a pro golfer, but he felt the most fun he had playing golf was when he was a kid. Growing up in San Diego, California, he was in an ideal climate for golf but he actually started playing in New Mexico. His grandfather had fashioned an old cow pasture into a golf course. He was only four and a half years old at the time so he emulated his father's grip and swing. Years later, when the family returned to San Diego, he got his first golf lesson. The first thing his instructor did when he saw his swing was change his grip to the Vardon grip.

By high school, Casper was shooting in the low 70s. But hitting shots on the range was never that satisfying to him. He preferred to go out to the course and play.

Casper caddied at San Diego Country Club and when his earnings helped him buy things he wanted, he decided he might be able to make a living at it. After one semester at Notre Dame and a four-year stint in the US Navy, Casper decided to pursue golf. Two local men were willing to sponsor him on tour, a boon for a young golfer. He played his first tournament in June of 1955, the Western Open. He tied for 30th place and earned $33.33. Thirteen months later, he won his first event. There were many more memorable wins to come.

In 1959 at the US Open at Winged Foot Golf Club in Mamaroneck NY, heavy rain and strong winds postponed the final round from Saturday to Sunday (back in those days, 36 holes was played on Saturday).

Casper went into the final round leading the field by three strokes. He felt confident. His approaches were good and he had been putting well.

Casper teed off in 40 mile an hour winds on Sunday. He focused on battling the course and the conditions not other players but it was difficult and he finished with a total of 282 (+2). A few holes back, two other players were closing in on his score while Casper could only watch it on TV from the clubhouse. One player fell away and another, Bob Rosburg, came up to the 18th needing birdie to force a play-off but he two-putted to finish one shot back. Billy Casper had won the US Open.

The win came as a bit of a surprise to Casper. He hadn't expected it so soon. He perceived winning the US Open as a crown jewel, one that would take him a long time to win. Despite feeling this way, he was already hungry for another US Open win. He didn't want it to be a one-off, a fluke, the height of his career. He was determined to get another national title. Ten years after turning pro, he won his second US Open at the Olympic Club in San Francisco when he beat Arnold Palmer in a play-off. But it wasn't just his golf prowess that led him to that second win. Casper had made big changes in his life.

A comfortable lifestyle had led him to overindulge in eating and he had ballooned to 225 pounds. His poor diet and subsequent weight gain led him to feel irritable, tired and he was plagued with chronic headaches. He eventually realized he had to change his diet or quit golf. He was able to get down to 175 pounds, a more fitting weight for his 5'11" frame. It took willpower but he succeeded and it improved his golf game.

Casper liked that in golf he had to rely on himself and not depend on a team-mate to do the work (or let him down). Golf exposes strengths and weaknesses. He didn't see himself competing against anyone other than the golf course, but he sure liked it if he beat the best players.

Mastering a round physically was just as important as mastering it mentally and Casper saw that as a personal victory. He also enjoyed the creative options in the game – like stepping up to a tee and deciding how he wanted to bend a ball around the obstacles on the course. He encouraged people to pursue the game because it was one that you could play your entire life and it would impact every aspect of your life, from physical health to mental strength and focus.

Because of what the game of golf gives to a person, Casper considered recreational golf a serious pursuit not a casual folly but my parents did not see it that way. I never argued or pleaded with them. I knew better than to do that

Little did I know that I would soon return to San Luis Rey Downs Golf Course.

*

I made a friend at school named Chelsea Vander and her family had a large beautiful house overlooking the San Luis Rey Downs Golf Course. One day, I went to visit her and she said she was tagging along with her father, who was going to play a round of golf. She wanted to know if I wanted to join them. My desire to go overwhelmed my fear of being recognized by that marshal so I agreed.

Mr. Vander had a giant cigar stuffed into his mouth when he drove off the first tee. Chelsea and I shared a golf cart while her dad played as a single ahead of us, weaving along the cart path. Chelsea wanted to talk about hair and nails and clothes and boys. I found those subjects boring and annoying because I wanted to fixate on Mr. Vander's game (such as it was). He swung at the ball like he was chopping down long grass. It didn't look pretty and after several swings, he finally made it onto the green. Three putts later, the ball was in the hole. I noted he didn't play like Vardon *or* Park. His game seemed laborious and not a whole lot of fun. This disturbed me.

On the second tee, he hit a slice and I tried to help him find the ball. When I spotted it, I picked it up and shrieked with glee. Mr. Vander came over red-faced and told me to never scream on a golf course and to "never touch the goddamn ball!" I dropped the ball, slammed my mouth shut and the smile disappeared from my face. He said the rough was lousy and he moved the ball to a better lie. It made me think that was how golf was played. Without a lesson or instruction, I thought you just moved the ball to a better lie whenever it was too difficult to hit.

After the rotund Vander sank a putt for par and seemed pleased with himself on one particular hole, I summoned up the courage to ask him if I could play golf. He looked at me, stern, and said, "This is a man's game." He wouldn't even allow me to touch his clubs or try putting an extra ball into the hole.

What he said was what I had heard all my life, so I began to believe it to be true. For one thing, there were no women playing on the course that day and Chelsea and I had been relegated to following her dad around in a cart rather than play. The only golfers I had ever heard of up until that time were men and I certainly could not swing the stolen 1-iron Tay had given me. It was made for a man, not me.

I got back into the cart with Chelsea. "What kind of work did your dad do?" I asked.

Chelsea was chewing on her ponytail. "Huh?"

"Your dad; what kind of work did he do?"

"Oh, he sells Ferraris."

"He's not retired?"

She frowned at me. "What? No, he's not retired. He's only like 40 or something. Old, but not *that* old."

I looked at her father, who was dropping a second ball after his first shot skittered into the unknown sphere of the rough. *So golf wasn't just for retired folks after all* as my parents had insisted.

I returned home more enlightened to the game of golf, but it did little good in getting me back out there to play. I had no equipment, no skill and worst of all no permission. I kept myself occupied by burying my head in *Golf Illustrated* at the library. It was high-brow journalism with intelligent prose and lofty phrases that made golf seem poetic. Each issue had an abundance of anecdotes that I found fascinating. On Harry Vardon it was written, "All his shots are tee shots. It was this that gave his game, but the true explanation of Vardon's success was his magnificent condition and sublime confidence in his own powers."

I gulped. I was certainly lacking in confidence. Did that mean I couldn't play? The only confidence I did possess was an overwhelming belief that I could play golf if given the chance. Was I delusional? I hadn't even figured out a way to get out there and play a proper round.

The magazine also addressed the addictive nature of the game which I was already experiencing. On golfing types, one article stated, "If you ask the first dozen golfers you meet to define the particular aspect of the epidemic from which they suffer, you will probably get a dozen different replies."

That was just how I felt; like I had a disease – a sickening, constant desire to play golf.

The article continued: "One revels in a tearing drive or a divine approach or the poetical inspiration of a ten-foot putt. Another finds it an adjusting medium for a terribly unpoetic liver. A third has never been around in a hundred and has vowed he will or he will expire in the effort. He dwells in a dreamland of inexhaustible possibilities. It grows every day like a mushroom or a fishing story and he sips nectar from the expansion."

I had yet to experience any of those things: a tearing drive or that divine approach, even that unpoetic liver. Still, golf was the greatest desire of my life.

It cost ten cents each to make photocopies of these pages and given the fact that I had no job and no allowance, I used my lunch money or money I found in payphones or on the street to make my photocopies of *Golf Illustrated*. It may have been easier to read them at the library, but I liked to read them while on my cot in the pantry because once I fell asleep, my dreams were all about golf.

The magazine also gave me my first golf lessons. There were photographs to aid in the instruction and these lessons became my most cherished photocopies.

"The speed should become constantly greater as the club-head comes to the ball, until it culminates at the moment of impact." That sounded easy enough to me. I was anxious to hit the ball anyway. *Who wouldn't want to get there as fast as possible?*

"The tendency of common men is to hurry to the swing." *Isn't that what they just said to do?* "Since this is a besetting sin…" *A sin?* "…the way to fight it is to aim rather at the opposite. Try to put the best pace at the moment that the club-head is an inch or two past the point at which it comes into contact with the ball. Our counsel is not for heroes but for erring men." They then recommended keeping an eye on Vardon's swing.

"Watching him may give a beginner a better idea of the meaning and value of correct timing than any pages of preaching."

I had no access to footage on Vardon so I had no chance of learning from his swing.

"Strictly speaking, it cannot matter what the club-head does after the ball has left it. We must recognize this and in recognizing this, it may be best to ensure the correct striking of the ball is by studying the correct way of the club-head movement after striking the ball."

I had no club, so I used my hand and a wadded up ball of paper to emulate the moment of impact and I could see that hitting my palm square launched a decent shot while closing my palm sent it left and opening my palm sent the wadded ball to the right. I did this until the librarian sternly told me that "spit wads are not allowed in the library." I shrunk down in my chair and slid my "golf ball" into my pocket.

I thought *GI* was a generous and helpful magazine to be giving me free lessons even though it was often stern in its delivery.

"It may occur to a beginner, who is capable of asking 'Why?' (and some beginners are capable of anything, even of this) that he does not see the reason for bothering so much about the way the club is brought away from the ball. The upward swing is easier to correct and criticize because it is or should be very much the slower."

This was an important lesson. I was not supposed to whip the club back and then whip it forward. Taking back the club slowly would give me the opportunity to get the club-face square just like I wanted.

"The reason we advocate this straight drawing away of the club-head from the ball..." *Yes? Yes?*

The magazine was torn in this area and I could not read the rest of the lesson. I was frustrated, believing that being able to read the rest of this column would give me a profound secret on hitting the ball squarely.

On the swing itself, there was a photograph of a man taking a half swing and then a photograph of a man posing at the top of the swing. This photograph shows a clear "chicken wing" at the top of the swing. This was embedded in my mind of how the swing should look.

I was happy to find, deeper in the issue, *Hints to Lady Beginners*. There again was a photograph, this time of a woman, in full dress, holding a driver at the top of her swing with a "chicken wing." She had perfect torso rotation, obviously aided it seemed to me, by that chicken wing.

In a column entitled *The Delirium of the Drive* I hoped to gain more knowledge on powering off the tee:

These lines are not intended to furnish a lesson, nor form a technical manual. The aim is rather to hint briefly and in a simple manner at some of the more important facts and laws of a tee shot. It has been proved that it matters little whether the left or right foot be advanced, a full or half swing taken, and that the exact tightness of grip and distance from the ball depends much on individual preference and conformation. What is of importance is how the club-head is brought away from and again down to the ball. This can be done on an imaginary straight line, extending from the ball to the player's right, and along which the driver should pass without any bending of the arms until the club is near the horizontal, pointing to the right. Long driving depends on clean hitting and following through as rapidly as possible.

Quickness and accuracy are acquired by mechanical repetition.

I was frustrated. I understood this instruction but had no club with which to practice. I stood up in the library with a ruler in my hand, trying to emulate the swing:

> Following through can be mentally visualized by another straight line, this time in front of the ball on which the club-head must continue to travel as far as possible. Let the club leave the ground reluctantly, because the object in taking it back is to put pace on when it returns again, and this cannot be done if the club is snatched away. After the ball is hit, swing easily. Try and make the arc of the circle which the swing describes as large as possible.
>
> The real beginnings of a first-class game lie in a good eye and the power of hitting. Long drivers reveal a physical tautness, strength, and command of muscle. In examining the nature and conditions of a long drive we find it evolves from a perfect circle, rapidity and power.

Right up to the current day this has been the most important and effective lesson for me. Proper contact between club-head and ball is what results in a good shot.

*

One Friday after spending hours in the library, I caught the bus to Bonsall and then walked two and a half miles home. When I got there, the house was in turmoil. Dad was hitting Mom and Mom was screaming at him. He was throwing her around the house, beating her up. She didn't fight back physically but she did fight back with words that cut deeper than a knife. I tried to wish myself away, but I couldn't move. I peed my pants in the middle of the living room.

When Mom saw what I had done, she flew over to me, grabbed my head and shoved my face into the urine, demanding to know what was wrong with me. I couldn't speak. I was too afraid and I didn't cry because I knew I would be hit again. But it didn't matter. Dad knocked me back and I was flat on the carpet. He stood over me and repeatedly punched me, my head whipping back and forth on the ground. Mom hovered, smiling from ear to ear, egging him on. During glancing blows I caught glimpses of Harry Vardon. In my hand I was clutching a photocopy of an article on him. His image stared back at me, blank and helpless.

The anger and violence had been triggered by the news that Tay had been arrested. Along with one of his buddies, Tay committed armed robbery at a gas station. He was on the run, briefly, before surrendering to the authorities.

When I returned to school Monday morning, I had a black eye and was covered in bruises. One of my teachers brought me into the principal's office and he asked me what had happened, why I had been beaten up. I felt ashamed about admitting that Tay had been arrested. I told the principal that I was to blame and that I deserved it. The principal was satisfied and let me return to class. It was later discovered that I lost 60% of the hearing in my right ear from that beating.

Several weeks later, Tay was sentenced to several years in state prison. Mom was bitter and angry. She wrote several letters to the judge demanding that he release her "innocent" son. Her letters were ignored. She took her rage out on me, beating me with a wooden spoon. Dad had fits of violence. I was terrified of both of them.

No one wanted to talk about what became of Tay except Mom. She blamed everyone but her son and told me and Belle not to tell another living soul that her son was in prison. I felt guilty and ashamed, humiliated and embarrassed; like the stink of prison was on me. If family members would call from South Africa, I would have to lie and say that Tay was out for the day and that is why he couldn't come to the phone. I couldn't bear to see a movie or TV show that was set in a prison. I still can't watch them to this day.

Every time I looked down upon the San Luis Rey Downs Golf Course, I didn't dream of playing golf anymore. I only remembered that day out with Tay and it made me feel sick to my stomach with shame. I had been there as a cohort with stolen clubs and a stolen round of golf, an example of Tay's blatant disregard for others. I felt guilty, dirty, a bad person. I was afraid I would also end up in prison. I wanted to die.

Years later, Tay was deported back to South Africa and I never saw or spoke to him again.

CHAPTER SIX

Golf, Girl

One day I came home from school and found the pantry had been cleared out and my cot was gone. My clothing was haphazardly thrown into a box. My precious photocopies of golf-related articles had all been thrown in the trash and were gone. I was devastated. They were my lifeline, my escape to a world beyond the life I was living. I was so upset, I sobbed uncontrollably. My father hit me hard across the back of my head. My senses were rattled and I staggered around the pantry, trying to steady myself. I tried to stop crying and bury the emotions deep within myself.

That was how I found out we were moving to a rental house in San Marcos, California.

Dad had lost all his money when the gold market crashed. He had never held a job and he was not about to go into the workforce. He was determined to realize his American dream on his own. The only problem was that Dad did not have a plan. The dream was the plan. He became involved in one get-rich-quick scheme after another, barely scraping by.

My dream continued to be to play golf, but it was not enough to keep me entirely distracted. I was deeply insecure about my parent's financial future. As a teenager, I began to worry about money every day of my life. I wanted to get a job. I wanted to get out of there like my sister Belle.

My parents had not brought my school records from South Africa which would indicate when I was due to graduate high school. Without records, the American school would not let me graduate. I had to spend another year in high school.

At the new school in San Marcos I ate lunch on my own and tried to keep to myself, but a small group of girls migrated over to me and we would talk. They were pleasant and serious about their schoolwork and their future. When one of them asked me what I wanted to do with my life, I timidly said I wanted to play golf.

"Oh, like that Babe woman," one of the girls said.

I didn't know what she was talking about but after school that day, I immediately went to the local library and inquired about "Babe" to the librarian. She gave me a book on Babe Ruth.

"No," I said, "Babe is a female golfer."

The librarian insisted there was no female golfer named Babe and essentially told me to get lost. I went over to the card catalog (there was no looking it up on line in those days) and searched for over two hours. I found nothing. I was also disappointed to find no copies of *Golf Illustrated* in this library.

I returned to school the next day to ask that girl more about Babe but learned she was out sick with mononucleosis. I couldn't wait for her to return to school.

Later that morning, I was in class, taking a test. The entire room was quiet. The teacher was standing in the back of the classroom so she could make sure no students were cheating on the test. At one point, she accidentally dropped a heavy book on the tile floor. I got so spooked from the loud noise that I shrieked and the pen in my hand marked right across my paper. I was shaking uncontrollably from the loud bang. The kids were laughing at my reaction. I looked from face to face as they guffawed at me. I had no clue why I responded that way. It made me feel like a freak. My shame deepened.

A few weeks later when the girl returned to school, I asked her the last name of this Babe woman. She didn't know. After harassing her every day for weeks to find out the name, she finally asked her father and he said her last name was Zaharias.

I went back to the library and found Babe Zaharias' autobiography *This Life I've Led.* I felt the need to go to the librarian and point out to her that this was the book I was looking for. She didn't remember the request or me.

I went into a corner of the library and read about this woman named Babe. She was a Texan, born to immigrants from Norway. Her maiden name was Didrikson. She herself claimed to have been named after Babe Ruth, but in fact it was just a nickname her mother (not into baseball) had given her.

From the get-go, Babe was an incredibly competitive girl and liked to compete at anything, even in sewing competitions, but such domestic occupations was a sign of the times rather than her passion. She wanted to compete in sports. She dropped out of high school and played basketball in Dallas. Ambitious, she also became a singer and harmonica player. She wanted to eat up as much life as possible.

Babe gained world fame in track and field and All-American status in basketball. She played organized baseball and was an expert diver, roller skater and bowler. She won two gold medals and one silver medal for track and field in the 1932 Los Angeles Olympics. The woman was amazing – a profound inspiration – and one of her biggest passions in life became golf.

She was a latecomer to the sport and competed in the Los Angeles Open, a men's PGA tournament, a feat no other woman tried until Annika Sörenstam, Suzy Whaley and Michelle Wee tried almost six decades later. Babe shot 81 and 84, and missed the cut. However, in that tournament, she was teamed with George Zaharias. They were married eleven months later, and moved to Tampa, FL where they lived on a golf course they had purchased.

Babe went on to become America's first female golf celebrity and the leading player of the 1940s and early 1950s. To gain amateur status, she had to play no other sports for three years, a difficult thing for a woman of varied interests. After gaining her amateur status in 1942, she won the 1946 U.S. Women's Amateur and the 1947 British Ladies Amateur – the first American to do so – as well as three Women's Western Opens.

In January 1945, Zaharias played in three PGA tournaments. She shot 76-76 to qualify for the Los Angeles Open. She then shot 76-81 to make the two-day cut in the tournament itself, but missed the three-day cut after a 79, making her the first (and currently only) woman in history to make the cut in a regular PGA Tour event.

Having formally turned professional in 1947, Babe dominated the Women's Professional Golf Association and later the Ladies Professional Golf Association, of which she was a founding member. She won the 1947 Titleholders Championship and the 1948 U.S. Women's Open for her fourth and fifth major championships. She also won 17 straight women's amateur victories, a feat never equaled by anyone, male or female.

While Zaharias missed the cut in the PGA Tour event during her first year of tournament golf, later, as she became more experienced, she made the cut in every PGA Tour event she entered. At the Phoenix Open she shot 77-72-75-80, finishing in 33rd place. At the Tucson Open, she qualified by shooting 74-81 and then shot a total 307 in the tournament and finished tied for 42nd. Unlike other modern female golfers competing in men's events, Babe got into the Los Angeles and Tucson Opens through 36-hole qualifiers, as opposed to a sponsor's exemption.

In 1948, Babe became the first woman to attempt to qualify for the U.S. Open, but her application was rejected by the USGA. They stated that the event was open to men only.

Zaharias wasn't dissuaded. She had her greatest year in 1950 when she completed the Grand Slam of the three women's majors of the day: the U.S. Open, the Titleholders Championship and the Women's Western Open, in addition to leading the money list. That year, she became the fastest LPGA golfer to reach 10 wins, doing so in one year and 20 days, a record that still stands as of 2012. She was the leading money-winner again in 1951, and in 1952 she took another major with a Titleholders victory.

Babe began to feel ill and played a limited schedule in 1952 and 1953. She was eventually diagnosed with colon cancer and after undergoing surgery, she made a comeback in 1954. She took the Vare Trophy for lowest scoring average, her only win of that trophy, and her 10th and final major with a U.S. Women's Open championship – one month after the surgery and while wearing a colostomy bag.

With that win, Babe became the second-oldest woman to win a major LPGA championship tournament (behind Fay Crocker). In addition to continuing tournament play, she also served as president of the LPGA from 1952 to 1955.

Babe's colon cancer recurred in 1955, and despite her limited schedule of eight golfing events that season, she managed to gain her last two wins in competitive golf.

On September 27, 1956, Babe Zaharias died of her illness at the John Sealy Hospital in Galveston, Texas, at the age of forty-five. At the time of her death, she was still a top-ranked female golfer. She is buried at Forest Lawn Cemetery in Beaumont.

Babe had lived every day to the fullest and never let anything hold her back. She also broke the accepted models of femininity in her time. Standing 5'7" tall and weighing about 115 lbs., she was physically strong but many derided her for her "manliness." She was not a beauty and many were offended not only by her looks but her desire to play golf.

Sportswriter Joe Williams commented, "It would be much better if she and her ilk stayed at home and got themselves prettied up and waited for the phone to ring."

Years later, Charles McGrath of *The New York Times* was kinder to Babe, noting, "Except perhaps for Arnold Palmer, no golfer has ever been more beloved by the gallery."

Women had been playing golf for decades, but the attitude toward female players was still tolerant at best. Back in 1903, writer Horace Hutchinson, in *The Guardian*, addressed the issue:

> "It is rather curious after a study and practice of golf extending unfortunately over thirty years to note the change that has come over the attitude of the golfing world towards women. Thirty years ago women did not play golf. They hardly played anything except the piano (and did so distressingly) or perhaps a little croquet with hoops about as narrow as a five barred gate. At one or two places exceptional such as St Andrews and Westward Ho (with its comparative modernity) women putted on

short courses with holes of a maximum length of not less than twenty-five yards. Sometimes they came with fear and trembling – perhaps with a sense that they were doing something a little fast. More than likely it was with a sense of fearful boredom to watch the greater game on the long links. It never seemed to occur to them as anything but a joke.

The first of the ladies that we heard to play golf regularly on a long course was Miss Chambers at North Berwick. But North Berwick then was not like the North Berwick of today. If the North Berwick of that day were shown to a modern lady golfer she would condemn it as altogether too short.

The first step in her emancipation from the putting green of the Victorian lady golfer was the compromise between the one club putting greens of the earlier period and the modern woman's claim to an equal right as men on the links of masculine dimensions.

North Berwick had very good ladies links at an early date so perhaps it was why Miss Chambers learned to play so well. So this was the beginning when ladies golf began to require a full swing and a full equipment of clubs. This taught the ladies golf other than putting. Then with the noble ambition that we all admire in them, they began to aspire to a golfing equality with men. Of course men here – as in other walks of life – for a long while resisted their claims and derided their ambitions. For a while, golfing woman walked on men's links more or less like a guilty thing with a consciousness of her vast presumption. But that did not last.

It became fashion for a short while to say that golf was not a graceful game for ladies; that the swing was not an elegant performance. That was said with a certain amount of conviction for a time and also contained a certain amount of truth. Even among men who have been used to other athletic games all their lives, grace in the use of a golf club was very rare unless the player became familiar with the game at a very young age. Most women had not been exposed to the game as youngsters. It was only the ladies who did not hold fast to feminine form who were able to achieve a proper swing.

There were still many who grumbled; there are even those who grumble still. They say that the women's links are good enough for women but not quite good enough for men. That is the point many critics of the woman golfer do not seem to grasp; that in censuring her, they are equally censuring themselves. The avowed ground of their grumbling is that women do not play well enough to be worthy of long links; that they block them up and impede progress. But they are quite good players, in many cases, as their critics. If the argument that inferior golf is not to be tolerated on long links were applied with any logic at all, it would remove a few of the male players as well. For many, it would be a very happy removal.

At all events, the question should not be one of gender, but of ability. A club conducted on these lines would be an innovation, indeed, but perhaps not a bad innovation. The idea has its attractions, but so far it is not taking shaping. In the meantime, women are modestly and graciously content in having established an equality of golfing rights with men. There are many links where that equality goes on unquestioned. Even at St. Andrews the starter calls out the names of ladies taking their turn with the men on the long links in a perfectly matter-of-fact manner (so accustomed to their presence he has become). It must shock the old school of golfers who have played many rounds here badly indeed, that they do not rise out of the bunkers and babble at them, trying to scare the women off the course., but the men never seem to do so.

All of this significant and highly successful revolt of golfing womanhood we have seen with our own eyes, achieved within the space of something like two decades prove women very well worthy of the victory they have won."

Babe Zaharias was clearly one woman who didn't let anyone or anything hold her back from the game of golf. She was not alone in her desire to be a competitive golfer who just happened to be female. Alice and Marlene Bauer had the same desire to compete, encouraged by their father, Dave Bauer.

Having arrived in Baltimore from a German settlement in Russia, Dave didn't even set foot on a golf course until he was 30 and living in South Dakota. The game soon took over his life and he was spending more time on the course than at his work as a restaurant owner. He bashed balls as if his life depended upon it. With instruction book at the ready, he would go out on the South Dakota prairie and hit balls, only stopping to review the book on proper technique. His self-instruction led him to a knowledgeable understanding of physics, particularly body rotation and follow-through.

Dave's passion for golf led to a job as the manager and teaching pro at a local golf course near Aberdeen. He was eager to have his daughters take up the game. Marlene began golfing at the age of three. Dave cut down a pair of clubs for her and began schooling her in the game. Alice, though older, only began taking the game seriously at the age of 11.

The family moved from South Dakota to California so the girls could play golf year round. Dave rigged up a platform that would make the ball drop out of position if Marlene lifted her right heel on the down stroke. He would make her repeat the swing until she got it right and Marlene's game began to steadily improve.

At the Los Angeles Women's Golf Championship, Marlene's scorecard noted: "No children under the age of 14 allowed" on the course. Thirteen-year-old Marlene hardly played like a child. She won the event.

After having worked at Douglas Aircraft in California, Dave managed a driving range for a while before becoming a teaching pro at Hollywood's Toluca Fairways, but he wanted his girls to be in the middle of the country so they would have easier access to nationwide tournaments. The family moved to Midland, Texas.

By the time Marlene was 16 and Alice was 22, their comely looks and precision golf set them apart from the regular female players who were considered less than attractive.

"I like the shorts as well as the shots," said one male gallery member at an event in which both daughters were competing, their shapely legs on full display.

Both girls had distinct personalities. It was reported that Alice was moody; high one minute, deflated the next. She would often irritate the gallery at how long she would take to hit a shot. Marlene, on the other hand, often wore a serene smile while competing. She seemed to ignore the galleries and played so fast spectators could hardly keep up.

The young women were pushed by Dave to practice relentlessly and he was not shy about pointing out their mistakes. They hit shot after shot until Dave was satisfied.

Dave Bauer was considered the driving force in his daughters' accomplishments and careers. It was rumored that he threatened them or belittled them and denied them access to normal teenage activities. The girls did not publicly complain and their mother always said, "Dave knows best."

While on break in between two matches at a Palm Beach tournament on a stifling hot afternoon, neither girl wanted to cool off with a shower because they feared it would tighten them up or worse, make them feel as loose as a noodle and desperate for sleep. Both girls frequently played exhausted, once having played eight straight days of tournament play without a break.

The media focused on their looks, but the girls had game. Alice could bomb a drive about 225 yards and Marlene could sink putts like no one else. Marlene was picked as Woman Athlete of 1949 by the Associated Press. She won the National Girls' Junior Golf Championship and became the youngest player ever to reach the semis at the National Women's Amateur Championship. At tournaments, she ranked ahead of Babe Zaharias on three different occasions.

Alice had a more modest career, having qualified for the National Amateur three times, but she did have a feather in her cap. In 1947, she beat golf great Patty Berg in an exhibition match in Long Beach where she broke the women's course record by shooting a 73.

At that time, the money was in exhibition matches and Dave hoped to cash in on his daughter's skills as long as he could prevent outside interests such as romance from hampering their game. Marlene was just starting to take notice of the men ogling her on the circuit and Alice said, "I never much cared for a boy who wasn't a golfer." She would end up marrying a pro golfer named Bob Hagge.

Alice never won on the LPGA Tour while Marlene accomplished 26 professional wins.

How competitive the sisters were about golf only they knew for certain, but an event did do serious damage to their personal relationship. Alice and Bob Hagge's marriage had produced a daughter, but Alice divorced him less than three years later on the grounds of extreme cruelty after Bob told her that he no longer loved her. A few months later, Bob Hagge got remarried – to Marlene.

"Naturally we don't like it," Dave told the press. Bob and Marlene would divorce nine years later.

In 2002, Alice died of cancer at the home of her sister, Marlene, so perhaps by that time, all was forgiven.

Reading about these women made a big impact on me. Being a female pursuing golf was not a weird, unusual or rare thing to do. I was not a freak or a wannabe jock or some course, uncouth female. I was a person who simply loved the game.

It was the first time I began to think that I could play golf – no matter what anyone said.

CHAPTER SEVEN

Hazard

During that last year of high school, I did a lot of walking. I had a physical sensation of something heavy weighing on my chest but also the sensation that a giant hole was forming in my torso. Getting out of the house helped relieve that sensation temporarily. I'd march down busy roads for miles until I was too fatigued to think. One day I was hiking down the road when I took a side street that led to a small agricultural field. There, beside the field, was a boy of about 14 years old with a rusty sand wedge in his hands. He was taking the club back half way and chipping rocks over rows of strawberries.

I hurried over to him, grinning from ear to ear. "Do you play golf?" I asked.

He looked sheepish and didn't speak a word of English. He only said, "Lee Trevino. Lee Trevino."

Lee Trevino had just won the 1984 PGA Championship at Shoal Creek and the kid was obviously happy and inspired by the win. Who could blame him? The flamboyant golfer was all over the news.

Trevino's story was really a miracle. He had a hardscrabble early life but was a hard worker and knew how to hustle. At age 17 he was in the U.S. Marine Corps where he played golf part-time with Marine Corps officers. He was later promoted to lance corporal. After his discharge four years later, he became a club pro in El Paso Texas and made extra money by hustling. His self-taught outside-in swing made his game unusually fun to watch. He could also talk up a storm to throw off his partner's concentration.

When Trevino qualified for the 1968 US Open, Sam Snead and Bob Goalby were watching him hit balls on the range. It was the first time they had seen the young Mexican kid from Texas. Goalby said, based on Trevino's swing, the kid would never last on tour.

Then, as it is today, many were looking for certain elements in a swing that made it "acceptable." By not setting up in a closed position (right foot and right shoulder are drawn back) or having the path of the swing close to his body like other tour players, Trevino's swing was considered unconventional. He had a slightly open stance with his feet aligned a little left of the target. On the take-away, his club came back along a parallel path with his stance. At the top of his back swing, his arms drew inward so that on the down swing, his right arm fell close to his right hip.

Trevino believed that you could stay out of trouble if you set up left and aimed right. It allowed him to keep his left hand square to the target and reduced the rolling over of the hands. Because he created his own swing, Trevino was suspicious of swing instructors. Trevino believed instructors were to be utilized to remind the golfer of the fundamentals: weight balance, stance, weight shift, etc., not to build a swing from scratch. Making perfect contact with the club-face was really the only proof of whether or not a swing worked.

Even after gaining success, Trevino's swing was still considered unorthodox. He joked that he didn't use video analysis because he had no desire to see his swing. But when he looked around during tournaments at the other players, he started to see that some of their swings were beginning to resemble his swing. By adopting his style, those players were getting tougher to beat.

He didn't think the way his swing looked even mattered. "If the ball goes where you want, it don't make any difference."

One of Trevino's most memorable wins was the 1971 US Open at Merion Golf Club, East Course in Ardmore PA where he defeated Jack Nicklaus in an 18-hole play-off. Lee earned an ardent band of followers known as "Lee's Fleas."

He loved his position in life. "You don't see Mexicans inside the ropes too often," he said smiling.

It was not the first time Trevino had mentioned his heritage. The year before at the Open Championship he was introduced to the British Prime Minister.

"Ever shake hands with a Mexican before?" he asked the country's leader, to which he got no response. The PM was thrown off by the remark.

Lee's win at Merion was not the only story that came out of the 1971 US Open. Playing quietly in that field was a conservative young amateur named Jim Simons. He rarely smiled, but he had poise and maturity that enabled him to get into the tournament lead in the final round.

At twenty-one years old with sun bleached hair and a boyish face, he stunned the field with his five under the card 65 in the third round. Simons doubted he would be able to sleep that night. Just the thought of facing Jack Nicklaus the next day made him tense.

"I've always dreamed of winning a US Open but I've never had the real confidence that I could do it. I would be much better off if I had a winning attitude," he said.

Simons would end up in a tie for fifth on that final day at Merion.

While Simons provided the on-course drama, Gary Player was providing off-course drama. Late on Friday afternoon, the USGA received a phone call from a man claiming to represent the Black Panthers. The anonymous caller threatened to assassinate Gary Player that night or "someone will get him over the weekend." The caller was apparently ignorant of Player's staunch position against racial inequality.

Federal marshals and local police guarded the private home where Player was staying in Philadelphia and accompanied him everywhere.

Player decided to stay at the tournament but refused to make a comment. His play seemed affected by the incident as he had a mediocre showing.

The event, however, ultimately belonged to Lee Trevino. The fact that he had beaten Nicklaus "the greatest golfer alive" according to Trevino was a thrill that stays with him to the present today. But Lee wasn't done. The Open Championship at Royal Birkdale Golf Club was coming up the next month and Lee would once again stand alone as the victor. He then solidified his standing in golf history by winning the Open again the very next year in 1972 at Muirfield after barely recovering from a bout of pneumonia.

He showed up that first day wearing a sombrero. Sometime before the event, Trevino said, "I'm going to play as much as I can, as hard as I can, win all I can by the time I'm 40 and then I'll go back home to El Paso and just sit and count my money. I'm going to have it stacked around the house in bales, not just bundles. I'm going to have it in bales and I'm just gonna sit there and count it and grin."

The loquacious star wasn't done voicing his thoughts. "I ain't gonna be out here trying to hack it around trying to beat the hungry kids. I sure as hell ain't gonna be a pro at some club somewhere and stand around sweating. That's not for me. I'm going to pile it up while I can. That's why I play so many tournaments. I've got a lot of other things going for me, but most of them are built on my playing golf and winning."

As to the venue, Trevino said Muirfield made him go to church. "You pitch the ball 30 yards short of the green and pray."

Before the final round at Muirfield, most bets were on Jack Nicklaus winning. Trevino was an annoying thorn in Jack's side since beating him at Merion and then taking the Open the year before in 1971, but Jack was coming off the Masters win in April and the US Open win at Pebble Beach and was in great form. He was the 9-4 favorite to take the Open and 10-1 to win the slam in the same year. Besides, he had won the Open at Muirfield back in 1966 when pros complained that the rough was so high "you had to get a search warrant" to find your ball. Now Muirfield was manicured and considered "gettable." The fairways, however, were still mercilessly narrow. As Sam Snead observed, "so narrow the dogs can only wag their tails up and down." But Jack couldn't hold off the loud-mouthed Mexican from Texas. Trevino once again took the Open title. Jack sat in second place just one shot back.

Trevino's natural talent and cunning game led to 89 professional wins, including 6 majors and being inducted into the World Golf Hall of Fame in 1981. That kid chipping rocks in the strawberry field had chosen a great golfer to emulate.

Over the next few months, I saw the kid several times on my walks and he appeared to be getting better and better at launching his shots. One day I saw that he had a bag of used golf clubs and a bunch of old balls. A chipping area had been fashioned out for him away from the rows of strawberries. The kid was on his way to perfecting his golf game. How I envied him.

I continued my long walks, dreading to spend any time at home. One day I stopped to rest near a new house that was near completion from construction. There, I met one of the construction workers, a 19 year old guy named Bobby. We chatted for a while and he asked me out. He said I better make a decision right then because he was moving on to his next project – working on the Fairbanks Ranch Country Club. When I heard he was going to be working at a golf course, I immediately accepted. He was perplexed when I asked that our first date be to go out to his job site at Fairbanks Ranch.

When I got home later that day, I realized I had accepted a date without ever asking my parents if I could go on a date. I was 17 years old at the time.

When I asked my parents if I could go out with Bobby, the scene was unpleasant. I had to beg and plead, suffer the slaps and punches, but the answer was a definite no. They said that I was selfish and only looking for sex like a "prostitute."

That night, lying in bed unable to sleep, I felt my first surge of rebellion. Rebellion takes a sort of blind courage to emerge and the only thing that was fueling that courage was my burning desire to go to the golf course at Fairbanks Ranch Country Club. I believed that Bobby was my way in and I would not let anything stop that.

The next day, I hurried back to the jobsite as Bobby was packing up to leave and told him to pick me up on Sunday. I gave him directions to a house on the corner where my parents could not see me.

The day of the date, my heart was pounding more about the golf course than the handsome young man who was going to be picking me up. When we got to Fairbanks Ranch, the club was immaculate, the fairways and greens the most alluring yellow-green. There was a sense of importance emanating from the clubhouse that seemed to confirm my belief that golf was the most serious and important endeavor I could undertake.

I nodded silently as Bobby blathered on about the construction project while I stared with mouth agape at men playing on the Ted Robinson designed golf course. They looked to be doing serious work, brows furrowed, lingering over their shots, thoughtfully writing on their scorecards. Naïve about the whole process, I asked Bobby if we could go play. He laughed and said the course was for members only. I asked him how much it cost to be a member and he said more than I could make "like in a hundred years." I was crestfallen, believing that golf was way out of my budget.

Bobby and I saw each other a few more times after that until he finally got tired of picking me up on the corner and spending the day at his job site staring at the golf course.

I finished high school and began to look for a job, hoping I could find work as a receptionist at a country club. That way, I figured, I could get closer to golf.

I continued to spend my free time in the library, reading all I could about the game. I particularly enjoyed stories about when golf was new to America.

When John Reid, an immigrant from Scotland, moved to Yonkers, New York, he ordered six golf clubs and two dozen golf balls. They arrived nearly two months later. Reid then invited some of his friends to join him in his cow pasture. They fashioned three golf holes by scooping out a handful of earth every hundred yards. There, Reid and a friend played what is believed to be the first game of golf in the United States.

Word spread and passion for the game grew across the country. Municipal courses began to pop up. The press took notice of the new sporting phenomenon, but more so for bad behavior. One editorial read: "The municipal golfer has little patience for the rules of the game and less for its etiquette. He may drive fearlessly into the next four-some and then proceed to chew up the fairways and greens with the grace of a wild water buffalo."

"It's risking your life to step off the first tee," said an attendant at New York's Pelham Bay Course. "It's like crossing an expressway during rush hour – only not safe."

Even highly-educated lawyers began to debate the matter:

"The space between the tee boxes should give no cause for angst but the badly driven ball brings about anxiety in the player. The thoughtful golfer sometimes ponders the momentous result when accidents are caused by the vagaries of his ball as it flies from the tee. Other players who are deaf to the cry of 'Fore!' find themselves not impervious to flying caoutchouc (natural rubber). What then are the legal liabilities connected with the game of golf?"

The law, interpreted by Dr. Bigelow, JD, as to injuries received in other sports was that it was a mutual combat of consent. But if the pastime is over and one player hits the other over some conceived wrong over the play then that is assault and battery.

Further, for those who tread upon the golf links hunting for lost balls (which had become a lucrative industry since the introduction of the Haskell and Kempshall balls), that offender is guilty of larceny.

The rubber-core ball was causing controversy not just for its cost and value. According to the *Chicago Post*, Harry Vardon wrote in a letter to a friend:

"The rubber cored golf ball has hurt the game. The ball makes my game six strokes better than the old fashioned ball on any course. A golfer loses full control of his game with the rubber-core ball. Shut your eyes and trust luck when playing with it. I sincerely hope that sportsmen will return to the good old Gutta Percha ball for which our courses were originally laid out."

Despite the controversy over the lack of etiquette and the golf ball material, all across the country, golf was gaining in rapid popularity. At New York's 10 municipal courses, it was reported that more than 22,000 rounds were played each week with weekend foursomes teeing off every six minutes. In Los Angeles, a staggering 962,474 rounds were played on 11 courses and the number was soon to top one million. Across the nation, it was believed that over 22.6 million rounds of golf were being played.

New York officials had to keep four of its courses open year round to accommodate the craze. Several cities wanted to promote that they had a municipal course, but many were substandard at best with fairways like concrete and greens that looked like badly mown weed patches. The majority of players could not afford to join private clubs, so they endured these jam-packed courses to their own personal discomfort.

To undo the jam of traffic and speed up play, municipal operators resorted to devious means, ingenious as they were desperate. At New York's Mosholu course, the rough was cut back to a minimum and sand traps were removed entirely. Los Angeles golfers were sternly advised by memo to "be ready to hit when it is your turn. Have ball, tee and club ready. Don't fumble for them at the last minute."

At Atlanta's Adam's Park, the officials removed all rest rooms in the playing areas to prevent dawdling. One newspaper noted: "Municipal golfers will abide any discomfort to get in just one round. Some of them are so fired up, they can think of little else."

Golf was becoming a nationwide addiction. A New York paper reported that at Brooklyn's Dyker Beach one summer, a regular showed up wearing swim trunks. "Oh, I'm in the wrong place," he said. "I was supposed to meet my wife at the beach."

Another story from Dyker Beach told of a woman who, on a winter's day, came out to play in a heavy wool coat. She just had to get her golf fix she said.

There were stories that foursomes gathered at three in the morning to play golf. One regular once apologized to his friends for arriving late to their weekly golf meet-up. "Sorry for being late," he said. "I got married last night."

Golfers lining up at midnight was standard on the weekends. Organized cook-outs took over parking lots. Night owls played cards, told stories or slept in their cars after having staked out their place in line. Players would often try to register their friends who were still at home while others had their wives or children wait in line for them. Once the club doors were finally thrown open, police had to be on hand to keep order.

Once, at a public course in Los Angeles, things got out of hand when people became professional line waiters, charging golfers up to $30 to take their place in line. The whole starting system had to be changed to prevent that. A golfer had to call for a tee time at least five days in advance and also had to buy an annual registration card. Each Monday morning switchboard operators would begin taking reservations for the following Saturday. However, since all of the preferred tee times were gone in 20 minutes, efforts were always made to beat the system. Businessmen had their staff come in early to work and had them flood the reservation department with phone calls to get a preferred tee time. Authorities discovered that golf nuts who worked for the phone company were making reservations by climbing poles and tapping into private circuits with field service phones. The women switchboard operators, who remained strictly anonymous, were offered mink coats, vacation trips and nights on the town in exchange for tee times. The clubs had to study lists to make sure none of their operators had given preferential treatment to anyone.

Images of golfers packing the putting greens at midnight or players battling inclement weather in five-foot high rough while staggering around from lack of sleep were splashed across the newspapers indicative of the golf craze. More often than not, however, once a quality golfer finally got to play a round, he was at the mercy of hackers and slicers or he was constantly nagged by players behind him who pressured him to hurry his shots. As if that wasn't bad enough, players would also fall victim to petty thieves in front who would pocket balls hit from players behind them. At Dyker Beach, banks of teenagers cut through the chain-link fence and hid in gullies to snatch well-hit drives. One gang of bandits brazenly threatened complaining golfers with bows and arrows. The superintendent couldn't estimate how many balls were stolen, but he did say they had to use over 4,000 feet of wire to repair fences.

On the 8th hole at New York's Split Rock, there was a man known as "The Fisherman" because he paid his way onto the course and then spent the entire day in rubber hip boots recovering balls that had been hit in the lake. At the plunking sound of a ball into the water, he would rise like Neptune, pluck out the ball and charge 25 cents to return it to the golfer.

At Chicago's Waveland course, the ball hawkers lined the fence that ran alongside the 7th fairway. A golfer who sliced one out of the park could not only buy back his ball for a small fee, he could arrange to "find" his ball in a preferred lie.

The maintenance problems created by swarms of players, most of them taking 100 or more swipes at the ball, gave green-keepers fits. The serious players were no problem. It was the tennis shoe players and the bag draggers that gave them the biggest headaches. An Atlanta pro said, "Some people pay $1.50 to play and believe they should get to take $1.50 of the course with them when they leave."

New York attendants had orders to keep mowing the green even when putters were holing out (a rule that created special hazards). At Split Rock, one mower was attacked by a golfer who blamed him for causing the golfer to miss a three-foot putt and when another greens-keeper removed the flag from the hole to do work, he became target practice for the approaching foursome. They were outraged at any delay or interference in their play.

Despite the crowded courses and all the characters that made playing golf arduous, the public kept coming back for more. Golf had taken America by storm and the game only strengthened in the decades to follow. Recreational players were keyed in on any opportunity to mingle with professional golfers.

In 1953, pro golfer Julius Boros participated in the Second Annual Golf Day Tournament. One hundred thousand golfers on courses ranging from Tijuana to Indonesia, regardless of handicap, entered the contest to try to beat Boros' score. Even Ben Hogan signed up to participate.

Around the world, players teed off en masse. Boros was playing at Oakmont near Pittsburgh. The 1952 US Open Champion played the dicey course well, barely uttering a word to those in attendance, and shot a 70. In order to qualify for the award, the competing players had to shoot lower than 70. By the close of the day, around 10,000 golfers were awarded a bronze medal with the inscription: "I beat Julius Boros May 23 1953." The award winners included the governor of Washington, a 5-star general, an 84 year old man, a 6-year old boy and two one-armed golfers. There were 14 holes in one. In Mexico, 500 of the bronze medals were awarded. Ben Hogan failed to win a bronze medal, but would be "the pro to beat" the following year.

Hogan, though a golf ambassador willing to participate in such an event was a very stern man. But then Hogan hardly had a soft upbringing. The son of a blacksmith who later committed suicide (reportedly in front of Ben when he was nine years old), the family fell into financial hardship. The three Hogan children all took jobs to help their mother, a seamstress, earn income. Ben caddied for a spell and began to play golf. He dropped out of high school and became a professional golfer.

He soon met the love of his life, Valerie, to whom he would be married to for 62 years until his death. Together they endured many years of little or no money on which to survive as Ben chased his dream.

One of the smallest men in professional sports at 5 ft 8.5 inches and never more than 135 pounds, Hogan practiced like a man possessed. He was known to spend hours on the range after finishing a round even when he was in the lead. Just one little flaw in his iron shots would cause him to blast away at the ball until nightfall.

By age 36 Hogan was the country's number one golfer but soon found himself in a hospital following an horrific car wreck. Initially it was believed he suffered three broken ribs and cuts to the face.

"Hogan is in shock," reported Dr. David Cameron from the hospital. "He is not unconscious. We are taking X-rays and should know the exact extent of his injuries later in the day."

Ben and Valerie were driving from Phoenix Arizona to their home in Fort Worth Texas after Ben had lost a tournament in a play-off with Jimmy Demaret. Valerie said she saw an approaching bus travelling the opposite direction from their car starting to pass a truck shortly before the accident. Her husband tried to avoid a collision but could not because of a culvert. The Hogan's vehicle crashed head-on into the Greyhound bus.

Valerie was not seriously injured and talked to reporters that afternoon. She said that her husband had thrown himself across the seat in front of her when he saw the collision was unavoidable. The impact pushed the engine of their Cadillac into the front seat. The steering wheel was driven into the back seat. Their luggage that had been in the back seat was piled on top of the couple.

News trickled out slowly on Hogan's condition. Some reports said he was fine and that all he needed was some rest while other reports indicated that he had suffered a broken arm that might impact his golfing career. His sister Carmelita said that the full report on his health was not yet complete. When it was finally known, the scenario was worse than imagined. Hogan had a double-fracture of the pelvis, a broken rib, a fractured clavicle, a left ankle fracture and near-fatal blood clots in his leg and lung. He eventually left the hospital 59 days after the accident but was in serious need of rehabilitation. He did so by extensive walking and returned to the professional circuit the next year.

Hogan admitted that he did not have the patience or temperament to be as affable as other professional players. Perhaps the near-death experience had caused him to want to accomplish as much in life as possible and it made him have little patience for smaller matters. Hogan, however, could have been considered a teddy bear compared to another young golfer who arrived on the pro tour a few years later – Tom Weiskopf, who one magazine called "golf's muscular heir apparent."

His fellow pros called him "Big T" but Weiskopf wasn't sure if that stood for his first name or his temper. He was an emotional player who "died" over every missed shot. He was picked by his colleagues to be the next Arnie or Jack – or, if he could not learn to control his emotions, the next Joe Divot.

There is a story of a golf promoter who located a 400 lb gorilla who could hit a golf ball 400 yards. The promoter set up an event where the gorilla would hit balls against Jack and Arnie. Before a gallery of 15,000, Nicklaus and Palmer both hit identical 275-yard drives down the fairway. Next stepped up the gorilla and WHACK! – a booming drive of 400 yards flew down the middle of the fairway and rolled onto the green five feet from the cup. Both Palmer and Nicklaus were shaking their heads when they hit their second shots onto the green. Palmer missed his putt but made his par four. Nicklaus curled in an 18-footer for a birdie three. Now here was the gorilla with a chance for an eagle two. The gallery fell silent as the hairy creature took his stance, crouched motionless over the ball then... WHACK! hit the ball 400 yards.

That was how insiders described the way Tom Weiskopf played golf.

The comparison of Weiskopf to the hard-hitting gorilla was light-hearted ribbing that stemmed from Weiskopf's enormous power. Once, Big T reached the 610-yard 18th hole at Upper Montclair with a driver and a 3-iron (considered impossible at the time).

In the New Orleans Open, Weiskopf found himself stymied by a palm tree, 200 yards away from the green. He decided to hit an 8-iron. The ball flew up over the palm and landed on the green. Weiskopf's caddie dropped the bag and fell flat on his back in the fairway, laughing. He couldn't believe it.

Billy Casper rushed over to Weiskopf and said, "If anyone had told me about that shot I would have called him a liar."

Arnold Palmer was also impressed and said, "The amazing thing is that the kid is stronger than he thinks he is."

Aside from his brute strength, Weiskopf was also considered a bit quirky and superstitious. He would never warm up on the range with woods.

"We worry a lot about Tom," said one un-named golfer. "We wonder if you look in Tom's ear whether you would see daylight or cartoons or something."

No one really knows how Big T felt about the ribbing, but it was well-known that he really liked to compete against Palmer and Nicklaus by unleashing one of his frighteningly long drives and watching his opponents' jaws drop.

Weiskopf played courses by feel instead of marking off distances. With Big T, you never knew what you were going to get, particularly with his mood. He displayed flashes of an unruly temper. Once, he slammed his wood against a tree and another time he yelled at his then-wife, Jean (who was innocently watching in the gallery) after he missed a putt. After a bad round in Orlando, he threw his ball at his caddie and said, "I quit! Pack up my stuff. I am going home." He went home for two weeks.

His caddie was publicly critical of him and accused Tom of being a "mama's boy."

"He hits a bad shot and you knew it was all over. You could guarantee he would bogie the next three holes. Then, he goes running home to his mother."

But in all fairness, Tom was very young and trying to cope with a fiery temperament that he had genetically inherited. It was a tough thing for him to manage. During his sophomore year at Ohio State University he dropped out until an upperclassman named Jack Nicklaus convinced him that his future was in pro golf. But Tom played badly in his first three professional tournaments and after the third event he announced in the locker room at San Francisco's Harding Park that he was done with golf. Several fellow pros talked him out of it.

A few weeks later, Weiskopf tied for 10th place in Tucson and finished in the money in almost every tournament after that. But his quirky behavior was not gone. Once, while looking over a putt, he backed right off the green and fell into a bunker. Another time, he hit a drive into a tree and the ball came right back and smacked him. Tom agonized over every shot and a doctor thought he had an ulcer.

Weiskopf listened intently to Nicklaus, who regularly delivered lectures on how to compose oneself on the golf course.

"When Jack gets on me, it really hurts," Weiskopf lamented.

One of those times was at Doral after Big T had made bogeys on the last two holes. Weiskopf stormed into the press tent and said that the marshals and the gallery had made him lose the tournament and that he would never play Doral again.

"The guy is a psycho!" one writer exclaimed, blaming Tom for not accepting responsibility for the way he played.

Big T had failed to explain why he felt the way he did. He had good reason to be annoyed. On the 17th hole, as he was getting ready to hit his third shot to the green, a marshal ran out and grabbed him by the arm.

"Dickinson (the tournament leader) has just hit it in the water at 18!" the marshal yelled.

Tom tried to pull his concentration together and again addressed the ball, but the marshal once again ran out and yelled, "Dickinson has just double-bogeyed 18! All you need is a par and a bogey to win!"

Weiskopf's concentration had been knocked off track. He hit his shot 30 feet short of the pin and two-putted for a bogey.

On 18, Tom's drive was in the fairway but in their rush to get to his ball, the crowd "ran over" Tom's playing partner, who happened to be his best friend. Big T was infuriated. He flew his second shot over the green and onto a sidewalk. He then chipped back but two-putted for bogey. He finished in second place and that is why Big T mouthed off about never coming back to Doral.

Nicklaus told him he should have just taken the money and kept his mouth shut.

"I can't do that!" Weiskopf said. "When I've got something to say, I say it."

Tom even blabbed about his fellow pros. Doug Sanders, he said, "wears girl's colors and bends your ear too much about his sex life." Snead, he said, "is rude and walks ahead of you a lot." Too many players, he continued, "play defensively and are just trying to get a check." On Hogan he said, "Ben plays so beautifully, he makes you feel like his caddie."

In 1973, Tom held the second round lead at the Open Championship at Troon but many were eager to see how the 43 year old Arnold Palmer would fare. Upon surveying the course, he said it "is drying very fast and getting almost like it was 11 years ago. The greens are excellent and I'm hitting the ball reasonably well."

His cheerfully cautious tone was a reminder of when Palmer came to Troon in 1962 as a dominant figure in the game. He tamed the course and his opposing players with a six stroke victory over Kel Nagle of Australia.

In 1973 hundreds of fans gathered just to watch Palmer practice. His sweet smile, twinkle in his eye and affable personality made him the fan favorite.

The press had the nerve to ask him about his eyesight while putting – given that he was now over 40.

"My eyesight? Well, I have glasses but I'm not going to wear them here. The putts up to 30 feet where I can see what I'm doing are the ones that don't go in. There is no trouble with putting (during practice). It's putting in the tournament that's the trouble."

Palmer said he was going to have two more practice rounds before the Open got under way and then "whatever happens, I'm going straight home."

Tom Weiskopf knew he wasn't as remotely popular as Palmer and acknowledged his flaws, but he did not think he could do much about it. He just wanted to win and win the 1973 Open Championship at Troon he did (his one and only major title).

My desire to play had all the intensity of Big T's fire. And my own temper was growing as I became intolerant of living in the oppressive environment that was my parents' home.

CHAPTER EIGHT

Out Of The Rough

I couldn't find a job at a golf course so I took a job as a receptionist at a high-end auto collision repair company. Our warehouse was loaded with Maseratis, Ferraris, Deloreans and Bentleys. I spent a great deal of time back there, fascinated by the design, engineering and luxury of the automobiles.

Work was a quick bus ride from the house we were living in so I worked long hours, overtime, anything I could to save enough money to buy myself a car. My boss thought I was the most ambitious seventeen-year-old he had ever met.

A few months later I bought myself a 1973 Ford Pinto for $450.

One day after work, I returned home dead tired to once again find my belongings thrown in a box. Mom and Dad had somehow come up with a down payment (later I found out it was from Grandpa) and bought a piece of property in rural Northern San Diego County. I went to work the next day completely distracted with how I could use their move as an excuse for me to stay behind in San Marcos. On my lunch hour, I went to see a number of apartment vacancies but could not afford the rent on my own and worse, no one would rent an apartment to a 17 year old. Since we were moving that very day, I did not have time to look for a roommate. I had to resign myself to the move.

After work I followed my parents up the twists and turns of the mountainous region of Northern San Diego County. When we finally arrived at the remote property,

I saw that it was a three-acre plot covered in orange trees that abutted an Indian Reservation. It was summertime and stifling hot; the orange grove not allowing any air circulation. There was no house, no structure whatsoever. Once again we were going to live in a tent with no bathroom, no electricity and no running water. My misery and shame and hopelessness of the situation overwhelmed me. In that moment I couldn't see beyond this miserable excuse for a life. I sat in my dinky Ford Pinto and screamed and cried with frustration.

Each day I drove forty-five minutes to work. Without a bathroom, it was difficult to get ready and be presentable for the high-end clients. An Arby's restaurant a block from work became my personal bathroom. I bought breakfast there each day so I could gain access to the bathroom.

I stayed at my job for twelve hours, not wanting to go back and sit in the middle of an orange grove. Every time I left work, I felt that heavy weight in my chest and an overwhelming sense of dread. To lift my spirits, I would try to imagine the day I would play golf.

On weekends, I hit rocks as far as I could, trying to launch them into the distance and imagine myself being carried away on the quartz and crystal. Life improved months later when Dad installed a septic tank and got a generator for some electricity. In the meantime, I was squirreling away as much money as possible. I got another job as a secretary that paid more money but it was more than an hour and a half drive away. There, I met a man seven years older than me, and we began a friendship that became a relationship.

John was funny and kind and protective and he thought the world of me. It was a new experience for me to feel loved and special.

One day I returned to the orange grove to find my parents in an emotional state. Two weeks prior, a neighbor down the road had yelled at Dad to slow down. Dad drove at a high speed on the short dirt road, blazing right past the guy's house, risking the lives of his young children and dogs. An altercation ensued and Dad told him to go to hell. Instead, the neighbor went to the county. Mom and Dad were living on the land illegally and the county was evicting them as squatters. Also, by then, Dad had not paid the mortgage on the land so even the bank wanted them gone.

Rather than deal with the situation through the proper channels, my parents abandoned the property and decided to return to South Africa. I refused to go, telling them that I was moving in with John. John was laidback and happy enough to do it so why not?

My parents fought me on moving in with John but the pressure of them having no place to live was too great so I finally got my wish. They returned to South Africa without me. I was free of them. I thought now my life would be happy and I would finally get to play golf.

I moved in with John, believing that I was finally an adult able to control and dictate my own life. I was wrong. In order to be a self-sufficient adult I had to work to pay my half of the bills to support our modest apartment in eastern San Diego County. There wasn't much time for relaxation let alone pursuing my dream of playing golf. I wondered if life had any enjoyment at all.

John was a baseball fanatic and soon, I was frequently going to San Diego Padres baseball games on the weekends because the company we worked for had box seats. It was a nice distraction but it was not golf. When I asked John about playing golf, he said golf was for "sissies" and there was no way in hell he was going golfing.

I was disgruntled. I was finally away from my parents and still I could not find a way to play golf or be supported in my pursuit of golf. There were no driving ranges, no large sporting goods stores and I didn't live within thirty miles of a golf course. I simply had no idea how to get started in the game.

One weekend in 1987 when John was out, I caught a glimpse of the Open Championship that was televised from Muirfield Golf Links in Gullane, Scotland. It was the first time I had ever seen Nick Faldo. I was mesmerized by the performance as I saw him win one stroke ahead of Paul Azinger and Rodger Davis.

Many Englishmen had won the Open but not since Tony Jacklin in 1969. The local press was elated over the Faldo win.

Britain and its former colonies often threw their support behind their compatriots. A year before the Jacklin win, when the Open was held at Carnoustie, the press touted the achievements of British golfers Brian Barnes and Michael Bonallack, an amateur, after they shared the early lead in the first round.

"I don't think I have been around Carnoustie under 80 before!" Bonnallack said, thrilled. But his enthusiasm would soon end after that first round. Ultimately, Gary Player went on to capture the title.

Watching that 1987 Open Championship was a revelation. The players' form was amazing to me, but also very intimidating. I knew there was no way I could ever play like them. I then briefly developed this silly notion that if I couldn't play golf, maybe I could caddie. I had read plenty about caddies and how they were as much a part of the action as the golfers themselves.

Back in the early 1940s, the PGA established new rules of etiquette for caddies all across America in response to what many considered was poor behavior by the bag carriers. In locker rooms, large illustrative charts were hung up for all the caddies to see on how to behave while caddying for a player. For instance, it was shown that a good caddie always carries the bag over his shoulder and away from the body to prevent the rattling of the clubs. There were instructions on how to properly wait for the player to hit his shot. The caddie was required to hold the rim of the bag, not lean on it or press against the clubs. Of course, how the player received the club from the caddie was crucial. Efficiently removed from a well-organized bag, the caddie was to hand the player the club with the grip toward the player and always, always must remember to remove the head cover from the putter. Caddies also had to stand at least ten feet away from the player as he was taking his swing and not offer unsolicited advice. Further, caddies were not allowed to sit on benches when waiting. The benches were only there for the players. During waits, the caddie was to remain silent unless spoken to.

The rules went on to emphasize replacing divots, how to man a flag and avoid being hit by the player's ball, but the greatest emphasis was placed on not swearing, smoking, horsing around, not practicing with a player's clubs and most of all, not mocking a player's shots. Well, I could certainly do all of that. But of course, caddying was not for me.

*

It was the late 1980s and we could only afford one small black and white television, but I was eager to watch another golf tournament on the rickety device. John became upset, yelling that he was not going to tolerate watching golf when he wanted to see the Padres away game. He changed the channel to the baseball game.

John simply refused to allow me to watch any golf. I wondered what the hell I had got myself into by moving in with him. I went into the bedroom to lie down and there began a tradition of spending every weekend holed-up eating and sleeping.

Life felt like a chore. I had no sense of enjoyment. Then one Monday morning, I had a difficult time getting out of bed. John had long since left for work. He needed to be there by 7:30 a.m. while I only had to turn up at 9:00 a.m. There was nothing to hamper my getting ready but I struggled to do the most basic things like brush my teeth and dress. I pushed myself to do every simple task. I grabbed my car keys and opened the front door. I stepped outside into the cool fall morning air. A crushing wave of nausea hit me. I swayed backward and gripped the door jam. I backed up into the apartment. I felt better in a few minutes. I stepped outside but again a wave of nausea overwhelmed me along with a sense of sheer panic. I had the delusion that someone was trying to kill me. I fell to my knees and crawled back into the apartment. I closed the door and almost instantly felt relief. I never left the apartment that day or for the rest of the week, telling my work that I was sick.

Financial pressure forced me back out of the house each morning. It was almost intolerable. I went to see a doctor and he gave me Valium. I took it each day, believing it would help cure me, but I just felt the same way except I was experiencing it in slow motion.

My work history became spotty and my relationship with John suffered as well. He spent a lot of weekends away with friends and that was okay with me because I got to be in the safety of our apartment and I got to watch golf.

John got promoted and transferred to the company's Riverside County location and we moved there together even though we were emotionally drifting apart. He was falling in love with his secretary at the time. I knew it but I didn't feel much of anything. No anger, no jealousy, nothing but fear about stepping outside of the house. I had zero confidence. Anyone who can't leave the house is a big fat loser I believed. I not only stopped watching golf, I stopped thinking about it. What was the point? It was never going to happen.

By 1993 I was so miserable in my life that I didn't want to live, but I just kept plodding along in a fog. John had moved on with his secretary and who could blame him? I did find transcription work that I could do from home and that helped ease the financial pressure I felt but it was hard to find happiness in the hot climate of Riverside County locked in a house all day long. Then one day (on one of my rare days out in the world) I actually met another man. The best part of all was that he played golf.

Joe and I moved in together in late 1993. It was a difficult transition. He was fifteen years older than me and had his own baggage, but there seemed to be a force I couldn't control propelling me toward him. With him I was able to step out more into the world but I always felt safest tucked away in the condo we shared together.

Every Sunday Joe got the newspaper and turned on golf. I sat next to him, beside myself with glee at the thought of watching golf with him. He mostly read the newspaper while casually watching while I intently watched the tournament shot for shot. I was exposed to the likes of Greg Norman, Fred Couples, Payne Stewart, Bernhard Langer, José María Olazábal, Ben Crenshaw and Seve Ballesteros to name a few.

Coming from South Africa, I had not watched a lot of television and I had no clue about the schedule, thinking golf was only broadcast on Sunday, so when I heard that golf was also shown on Saturday, it became appointment viewing television for me on both days. Joe and I usually watched together, but sometimes he would leave me and go play golf with his friends. I would watch him leave, envious, but I didn't express my desire to golf. I still was getting to know him and he could be quite stern at times, so it was hard to approach him about something so important to me.

Joe liked to do some travelling so I agreed to go. It was the most difficult thing I had to do. I would get sick before every flight and the only way I could pull it off was to not sleep for several days so that I was just too exhausted to feel that amped anxiety. I rarely enjoyed any of the trips. I just wanted desperately to get back home.

In 1996 I agreed to go to Vancouver Canada. On the flight up, Joe was in a good mood. I don't know what prompted it, but I suddenly asked him if we would ever golf together.

Joe turned to me, quizzical and said, "No."

I was shocked. "But why?"

"I take golf very seriously," he said.

I didn't argue, pout or complain. All my life I had heard "no" when it came to golf. What else was new?

Vancouver is a gorgeous city and we went there in perfect June weather, eating salmon, sightseeing and enjoying beautiful scenery. I felt relaxed and happy – a trip that was nothing short of perfect. As we were walking around the vast and lush Stanley Park, Joe suddenly asked me if I wanted to play the park's short Par 3 course. I had never heard of a Par 3 course, but I jumped at the opportunity to play. I was out of my mind with excitement.

The attendant gave both of us a wedge and a putter and off we went. I was wearing a sundress and sandals. I was doing my best to emulate the golfers I had seen on TV. Most of the balls I hit skittered along the ground onto the green. I could not launch my shots beautifully like Joe, but I was happy and having fun. Joe was focused, serious and studying every green like it was the winning putt at a major. I didn't think much over a putt. I just went up and hit the ball in the hole. By the end of the nine holes, I had beaten Joe. He was not upset, but he was not happy. I turned to him and said, sheepish, "I'm sorry. The ball just kept going in the hole."

I replayed those nine holes in my mind over and over again on the flight home. Joe was a fairly good golfer (12-handicap) and to be able to beat him, even on that simple track made me gleeful.

Joe said I would need to take lessons if I wanted to play golf. As much as I loved the pitch and putt in Stanley Park, once we returned home I fell back into my fear of leaving the house. I had no courage to go out and take lessons. We also lived in a very hot part of Riverside County and for much of the year it was unbearable to be outside. I resigned myself to the satisfaction I got watching golf every weekend in our air-conditioned condo. It was safe and secure. I was still living off the high of my "victory" in Stanley Park. Besides that, it was an exciting time to be watching golf.

CHAPTER NINE

Uphill Lie

The young Tiger Woods was a fascinating player to watch. I was enthralled by his performance at the 1997 Masters. People who didn't pay that much attention to the game were suddenly drawn in by the phenomenal young golfer. Many ignorant to golf history believed that Tiger was the first black golfer, but that wasn't true. During a much more difficult time – the civil rights movement – African-American men and women were trying to make their way through the golf ranks. One of them was Calvin Peete.

Calvin had his own personal challenges to overcome in addition to dealing with racial inequality. His left arm was crooked after Peete fell from a tree at the age of 12 and fractured his elbow in three places. But that was about the only thing crooked in Peete's game. He could drive it long and straight and regularly ranked high in hitting fairways and greens even though he did not begin playing golf until he was in his twenties. He took to it quickly and immediately began excelling. Even he was surprised by his success because it all began as a lark.

Peete was one of 19 children born poor in Detroit Michigan before the family moved to Florida. He dropped out of grade school to go work in the agricultural fields with his father. The work was hard and demanding with low pay. Peete felt it was demeaning to him as a person and he became determined to get out of the fields. He decided to sell goods to the migrant field workers rather than be one of the migrant field workers. By the age of 17, he was self-employed and bringing in about $200 a week. From there, he took his money and slowly began buying rental apartments.

When Peete was 23 and in Rochester New York still selling goods to migrant workers, a couple of guys he knew invited him to come out to a public course and play golf. Amused by the offer since he had never even held a golf club before, Peete joined them. It was enough to get Peete hooked on the game.

When he got back to Florida, he bought his own clubs and practiced diligently. The first time he played 18 holes, he shot 87. A year and a half later, he broke par. His buddies didn't understand how he could play with a crooked arm. The supposed rule in golf was to have a straight left arm when taking back the club. Peete saw the hinge in his left arm as an advantage and allowed him to make fewer mistakes.

Besides a sun-up to sun-down practice routine, Peete also read instruction books and studied sequence photographs of his swing that he had taken himself with a motor-driven camera mounted to a tripod. He felt that he could learn more by watching his own swing and making adjustments from what he saw. He did take one lesson from golf instructor Bob Toski after struggling with his short iron shots. But overall, he taught himself.

When Peete saw how much money pro golfers were making in the mid-1960s, he made it his goal to become a professional. He wrote down a series of steps that he would take to make it on tour, but Peete was overly ambitious. Practicing and playing golf on the public courses was very different from tournament golf. Playing in front of a gallery also brought on extra pressure. Only by the age of 36 did he finally become accustomed to playing the tour. He won his first championship and was regarded as a player who was there to stay, even drawing compliments from none other than Jack Nicklaus.

Peete won four times in 1982, finishing fourth on the money list and would go on to accumulate 14 professional wins. In 1984 he was awarded the Vardon Trophy by the PGA of America for the leader in scoring average and the Byron Nelson Award presented by the PGA Tour for the player with the lowest adjusted scoring average for the year.

The best Peete performed in the majors was a tie for third in the 1982 PGA Championship and a tie for fourth in the 1983 US Open. The year Jack Nicklaus won his last major, the 1986 Masters, Peete tied for 11th.

Calvin Peete credited golf for getting him out of life as a field worker, but it was really his strength of mind and determination to be better and do better for his life and his family that propelled him. "Whatever you do," he said, "you must dream of success to be a success."

At the age of 39, even after all of his financial success, Calvin Peete passed the equivalency test to become a high school graduate.

*

Althea Gibson, an African-American tennis player, also became a professional golfer. She took up golf at the age of 32 and turned pro four years later. Wanting to stay in sports, she felt golf was a good choice, but the ladies' pro tour didn't pay much. A couple of doctor friends sponsored her and a jewelry store owner once backed her to the tune of $300 per week for 90 days. It was barely enough to cover room and board and if she took a plane, she was in the red, so she drove a lot. Airlines were interested in shelling out money to Jack Nicklaus and Arnold Palmer, not supporting a female player on the ladies' circuit even if she was a well known former tennis player.

Gibson could have just stayed home. She was married to a man who provided a decent living for the family and she admitted there was no way for her to actually earn a living on tour. "We put in as much time and work as the men do," she said at the time, but the interest was simply not there on the part of sponsors or fans.

"Althea might have been a real player of consequence had she started when she was young," Judy Rankin said. "She came along during a difficult time in golf, gained the support of a lot of people, and quietly made a difference."

On the men's side, there was also the tough and remarkable Charlie Sifford, the first African-American man to earn his PGA Player's Card. The press referred to him as a "cobra with veiled and deadly eyes." His face was somber, hostile even, his thin dark moustache adding to his mystique. An inch thick cigar usually jutted from his mouth. But despite his visage, Sifford was gregarious and humorous and went about his trade with gusto.

Sifford fought hard to play on tour, facing many pitfalls and disasters. Few were welcoming to a black golfer, but whenever he could get into a tournament, he plopped down his bag and went for it. Success was not instantaneous and he became bitter, angry and frustrated. He had a wife and kid to support and he was feeling the pressure. There were many lean years before he was able to break through and make some money that would give him a comfortable lifestyle.

In 1955, Sifford shot a first round 63 in the Canadian Open. Arnold Palmer had shot 64 that day. When Palmer came rushing off the course expecting to see his name at the top of the leader-board, he shouted, "How the hell did Charlie Sifford shoot a 63?"

Sifford was standing nearby and said, "The same way you shot a 64, Arnold Palmer." The two laughed and became fast friends.

As late as 1964, Sifford was still being ordered off of golf courses, even though the PGA had dropped its color ban in 1960. Most security officials and marshals ordered him off the course because no one believed that he was one of the pro players.

Sifford went on to accomplish 21 professional wins. In 2004, he became the first African-American inducted into the World Golf Hall of Fame. He chose fellow Hall of Fame member Gary Player to present him for induction. On June 22, 2006, he received an honorary degree from the University of St Andrews as a Doctor of Laws. He also received the 2007 Old Tom Morris Award from the Golf Course Superintendents Association of America, GCSAA's highest honor. In 2009, the Northern Trust Open created an exemption for a player who represents the advancement of diversity in golf; it is named in honor of Sifford and is referred to as the Charlie Sifford Exemption.

*

Pete Brown was the first African-American to win a PGA Tour event. He showed promise early on. He took up the game at the age of 15 when he became a caddie. He would do his loop and then go out and play a round or two. An oil executive he worked for named Jim Vaughn saw how well Pete played and loaned him clubs. At the age of 18, Brown was hired as a salesman at the club's pro shop and received his first lessons from a golf instructor. As a 19-year-old, he entered the Lone Star Open in Houston (an African-American event). He claimed first prize and beat the tournament's star, Charlie Sifford. But like Sifford, he also found sponsorship difficult to come by. His talent continued to make news and Detroit businessman Randolph Wallace offered him a contract. Pete accepted and happily went north, but found on his first day in the big city that blacks were not allowed to use public courses. On his second day in the city, he couldn't play at all. He woke up with a stiff neck and was told by a doctor that he had strep throat. But his legs began to weaken and his fingers became numb. A final diagnosis was infectious mononucleosis. He had to spend the next year in a Detroit hospital. During that time, Pete suffered with suicidal thoughts. He couldn't play golf; in fact, he couldn't do anything. He felt he had no reason to live. But he did not give up and followed an intense physical therapy course. By 1957, he had full control of his muscles and the hunger to play golf. He played in several events, but lingering weakness left him out of the money.

Pete won the Michigan Open and though it was not a PGA Tour event, Pete seemed to be on his way to a full-time career. Unfortunately, Randolph Wallace died and Pete was back without a sponsor and dead broke during the most critical time in his career. Discouraged but hopeful, Pete headed for Los Angeles. There, he met a prominent physician and after a few rounds at the Fox Hills Country Club, Pete had a sponsor again. Then he put his foot on the gas. At the Waco Turner Open in Burneyville Oklahoma, he became the first African-American to win a PGA event. It was a great boost to him and he went on to finish well at several tournaments to follow.

Brown was plagued by a back injury at one point, but he kept on pursuing his career. He would go on to accumulate 14 professional wins.

*

Pete Brown and Charlie Sifford never got to play in The Masters. That distinction of being the first African-

American to play at Augusta went to Robert Lee Elder but it was a bumpy ride. To begin with, Elder was outraged when he was quoted in the press as calling the tournament "racist." He said he had been misquoted. The piece alleged that Elder said he was kept out of the event because Clifford Roberts, the chairman of the Masters at the time, preferred the color of lily white. It was rumored that Roberts said that as long as he lived, the Masters would have nothing but black caddies and white players. Further, the article claimed that Elder thought all the new convoluted rules and regulations were deliberately set up to keep out black players.

When confronted with these supposed comments, Elder denied it and would not publicly charge the Masters' selection process as discriminatory. The Elder camp tried to impress upon the media and public that Elder considered the Masters just another golf tournament, but everyone knew it wasn't. It was special and many suspected Lee had a burning desire to play the event.

Leading up to the tournament, Elder received an avalanche of hate mail. Fearing for his life, during the week of the event, he rented two houses in town and kept moving between them. Elder shot a 74 on day one and a 78 on day two of the 1975 Masters, missing the cut, but the impact of his presence at the tournament was significant. The racial barrier had been shattered at Augusta.

Most of Elder's sponsorship came from the United Golf Association (UGA), an African-American organization. Long before gaining that support, at the age of 15, Lee was a caddie in his native Dallas. He learned so fast that a year later, he played well enough to finish second in the UGA finals.

Drafted by the U.S. Army, military service actually polished Elder's game. He was assigned captain of the golf team at Ft. Lewis Washington and they provided him with constant competition from nearby college teams. After his discharge, Elder taught at the Langston Golf Course in Washington D.C. After bagging several tournaments, he debuted as a pro, winning the UGA National.

The PGA tour had tough entrance requirements, requiring players prove they could finance over $6,500 worth of expenses for six months. That was considered a lot of money back in the late 1960s and Lee could not fund it. He instead played where he could and amassed a staggering 18 wins out of 22 tournaments.

Elder raised enough money to attend qualifying school for the PGA Tour in October of 1967 and played 18 holes a day for eight straight days. He finished 9th in his class, proving that he was ready for the big time. Elder was eager, saying, "I will play every time I can, every place I can."

In 1968, writer Louie Robinson called the Jack Nicklaus/Lee Elder duel at Firestone Country Club in Akron Ohio on a hot August Sunday afternoon a battle of "David and Goliath. Nicklaus and Elder swung irons as if in mortal combat." Elder took Nicklaus to the fifth hole of sudden death before losing, but the event raised his profile significantly. It inspired him and he went on to finish in the money for nine straight tournaments, a PGA rookie record at the time.

However, Lee Elder was not spared from racial backlash. When he was leading the Memphis Open one year, some kids scooped his ball off the green and were making off with it when Elder yelled at them to drop it. Hearing him, the youths instead threw the ball into some hedges 20 to 30 yards from where it first landed. The ref allowed Elder to take a fair drop, but it was believed the ball was taken because many did not want a black man to win the tournament. He was constantly harangued by unruly members in the gallery and Elder went on to take second place.

Though Elder never won a major, he was one of the trailblazers that would open the door to players of all ethnicities.

The emergence of Tiger Woods was exciting to watch unfold on television each weekend in our condo. Joe would often be gone playing golf, but I couldn't leave my secure environment.

It was hard to admit, but now the only person holding me back from playing golf was me.

CHAPTER TEN

Teeing It Up

In 1999 we left southern California when Joe took a position on the central coast of California. Not only would we be living in a cooler climate, we would be moving closer to the area that I believed was the Holy Grail of Golf – Pebble Beach.

Joe's friend Jim Gallagher, an ex-surfer, ex-firefighter, wine aficionado and all-around raconteur put on an unforgettable wine dinner soon after we arrived. Also at the dinner was Jim's brother Mike and when the subject of golf came up, conversation turned to a golfer named George Archer.

Born in the Bay Area, the nearly 6 foot 6 Archer was a hero to many local golfing residents. After he won the 1969 Masters, the 29-year-old declared, "This is George Archer" as if to say that winning such a prestigious event was synonymous with who he was. But Archer insisted that winning hadn't gone to his head.

"I'm just going to stay on the tour and slug it out. I haven't changed."

With a high-pitched voice and an uncanny resemblance to television character Gomer Pyle, Archer said that to win a tournament you had to get every good break. He had emerged out of the pack on that crisp and cloud-covered Sunday in April after battling for the lead with Tom Weiskopf, Canadian George Knudson and Billy Casper.

Casper, who shot a final round 74, was dismayed. He had led or shared the lead for the first three rounds. Casper managed to make five bogeys in a seven-hole stretch. "Golf is a humbling game," he said later. "I learned a lot of humility on that front nine."

Former Masters Champion Charles Coody had also made a charge, even holding the lead at one point, but bogeyed the last three holes.

During the tournament, Archer fluctuated between thoughts of winning with thoughts of trying not to do anything stupid. On the 15th hole, he managed to make par after having placed his second shot right into the water in front of the green. He pitched on and then holed a downhill 13-foot putt for par. That steadied his play. He went on to finish the rest of the round with consecutive pars to secure the victory.

When defending champion Bob Goalby slipped the green jacket on Archer's shoulders, the lanky Bay Area resident grinned. "I didn't think they had one in my size."

The press asked exactly what was his size and Archer replied, "Forty-two, extra long." And his shoe size? Archer shook his head. "Those are made by a boat-building company."

Health problems plagued Archer, which was difficult for him to cope with given the fact that he wanted to just go out there and tear it up. It was reported that he had abdominal pain for a while after the Masters win and then had calcium deposits in his left elbow.

"It got so bad that I couldn't lift a club," he said. "You just can't play good golf without a solid left arm. Now that I am on some pain-killing medication, that seems to do the job."

After winning the Andy Williams-San Diego Open two years later, Archer remarked, "You can't play well if you're not healthy. It's been a long time but I feel fine now, just fine."

He also attributed his win to a beaten-up golf ball, his tattered red sweater and the fog hugging the Torrey Pines Golf Course. The former ranch-hand admitted to being superstitious. The golf ball and his red sweater had both been used during his Masters' win.

As for the fog, it didn't bother the San Francisco native. "I won my first tournament in the fog."

In 1972, after losing the Glen Campbell-Los Angeles Open to Archer, fellow pro Tommy Aaron mused, "It's impossible for George Archer to make a bogey."

Considered one of the best putters on tour, Archer went on to hold the PGA record for making the fewest putts (94) over four rounds.

Three weeks shy of his 45th birthday, Archer won the Bank of Boston Classic in 1984. Winning then "was a lot better than shooting pheasants" Archer said at the time. "I had goose bumps on the back of my neck." He had won by the biggest margin of his career. "Perhaps I'll be around for a few more years."

Archer accumulated a total of 44 professional wins but the greatest win of his life was probably meeting and marrying his wife Donna. Together they shared a secret. George was illiterate.

Archer was anxious throughout his career about his inability to read. He was even reluctant to return to Augusta for fear of being exposed if he had to read some prepared statement to the press.

In 2005, at the age of 65, George succumbed to Burkitt's lymphoma, one month after playing his final round of recreational golf. His wife, Donna, was right there with him at the end.

"I was holding him and it was a beautiful experience," she said. "He was quite expressive about what a wonderful life he'd had, to be able to have that kind of career. He was on the tour for 40 years."

In April of 2009, Donna Archer walked The Masters course from the 18th hole backwards, celebrating the 40th anniversary of her husband's victory.

Perhaps George Archer knew how many Bay Area residents supported him, perhaps not. Either way, I was thankful I had learned about a man who may otherwise have been lost among the big names in the world of golf.

*

Despite the appeal of a new life on the California Central Coast, I still could not get out of the grips of agoraphobia. We had a beautiful view of the Monterey Bay and that allowed me to breathe in the beauty of nature rather than be boxed in with four walls, but I still couldn't venture beyond our property. I battled each day to take those steps out of the house. The big move itself had nearly killed me. Now that I was here, I still couldn't break out of my mental prison.

The bright spark, as always, was watching golf. When we got the Golf Channel on cable, I thought I had died and gone to heaven. All golf, all the time was a dream come true, but it kept me locked inside my safe world.

I spent the next several years at home, venturing out on rare occasions but only to quickly return due to a horrendous panic attack that would embarrass me and Joe. I went back on medication and began to talk to a professional. He believed I had PTSD from my childhood. Whatever the source, I was sick of being this way. I was screaming in my head, "Stop this madness! Get outside. Do it!" but my feet wouldn't move.

People have gone through much worse than me and they didn't cower in their homes. Cowards can't live a full life and cowards certainly can't play golf.

A man named Dennis Walters was no coward. He began playing golf at the age of eight and was hooked on the game. Then one day, while driving an old three-wheel golf cart down a steep incline, the cart toppled over, landing Walters onto his lower back. The freak accident left him unable to walk.

Walters wasn't just a recreational golfer when the accident occurred; there was promise of a golfing career. He had won the NJ State Junior Championship and placed 11th in the US Amateur Tournament and missed qualifying for the pro tour by eight shots.

For a while, Walters believed that he would walk again, but soon it became apparent he would not. After long months of physical therapy and rehabilitation, he was determined to find a way to play golf. A custom-built golf cart was the answer. Walters hit his golf ball half-sitting, half-standing while on the edge of a seat that flipped out from the side of his golf cart. A seat belt was fitted around his waist to keep him from falling over.

Walters began to travel the country, giving demonstrations and inspirational talks. He even got his dog, Mulligan, into the act. She teed up the ball with her teeth. Soon Walters became a highly-acclaimed trick shot artist. He could swat the ball with a hose, a baseball bat, a crutch and even a fishing rod.

Four years after his accident, in 1978, Walters earned the Ben Hogan Award as the comeback golfer of the year. He is one of only a few men who have been named an honorary lifetime member of the Professional Golf Association of America.

Walters kept up his positive outlook on life, saying, "I try to point out to people that maybe there is something in their lives that they would like to do that maybe they think is impossible or people have told them is impossible. But I say that if you work at it, persevere and hang in there, you can achieve success at almost anything."

LPGA member Kathy Linney was no stranger to perseverance. Cancer tried to stand in the way of her career when she was just 23 years old, but she battled her way through it. She worked part-time jobs while trying to make it on the LPGA tour and once she made it, she then had to battle recurrent cancer and extensive surgery. Linney said that battling cancer was a lot like playing golf. It was about one day at a time, one shot at a time.

Fellow pro Catherine Duggan praised Linney as a fighter, saying she was an inspiration; not a sad sack story. "She makes you want to go out and move mountains."

Kathy Linney died at the age of 36 after a ten year battle with cancer. She remained active in golf until the very end.

I didn't have loss of limbs or threat to life, so I felt foolish. I read plenty of examples of people overcoming hardship yet agoraphobia was the greatest battle of my life. I had spent a total of 11 years unable to leave the house. The only thing slightly stronger than agoraphobia was my burning desire to play golf and that desire would not be denied. I was feeling intense frustration when Joe would leave to play golf. Why couldn't I go?

"Well you won't leave the house!" he yelled.

Finally, I had enough. I demanded he take me golfing. Joe said fine but he doubted I could set foot outside the front door. He insisted that if I was serious, I would need golf clubs and some golf lessons. I resentfully agreed to lessons, thinking that doing so would only delay my long-awaited desire to play golf.

It took Joe weeks to find a combination of used ladies clubs to buy on Ebay. When they arrived, they were too tall for me so Joe cut them down and re-gripped the clubs while I hovered over him. He insisted we weren't going anywhere until I took some lessons. In the meantime, we would go to the local range to hit balls. To do this, I was able to leave the house without a problem.

Joe gave me some basic instruction on the proper grip and stance but it was difficult. I had developed my "swing" out of hitting rocks and that motion was useless for golf. I had to break out of a sweeping motion and instead hit down on the ball. It was difficult. I hit shots in directions that made no sense, once hitting the person right next to me on the range. The most frustrating aspect was I couldn't get one ball up in the air except for the driver. It was impossible for me to hit the 3-wood or the 5-wood. I had better luck with a 9-iron but the ball was shanked. Joe was right. I went into the clubhouse and signed up for three lessons.

Sam Snead once said that not even taking countless lessons was going to help a beginner because most golfers feared the ball:

"Ever see someone stand over a ball for 45 seconds or back away repeatedly and then stand over the ball and glare at it again? Or on the first tee in tournament play, nerves can run so high it takes two hands just to place the ball on the tee? Fear creates tension and that rankles the golf game. When your mind begins to unravel, your round spirals out of control. You feel like you are in a dark tunnel with barely enough oxygen and people are watching you and perhaps even laughing at you."

I was haunted by Snead's words. It was ridiculous, I told myself, to feel like I had to "perform" when I was just a beginner. On my first lesson, the teacher, a female instructor, was friendly and direct, but I felt no inspiration. She told me first to swing the club without force, just naturally. I did so and completely whiffed it.

"Keep your eye on the ball," she said.

I chuckled. I knew keeping my eye on the ball was not entirely necessary.

Many years ago, a golfer named Charles Boswell shot a 39 on nine holes at Highland Park Course in Birmingham Alabama. Upon hearing about this, a sporting goods company presented Boswell with a set of matched clubs. Golfers in Birmingham said they were going to quit the game and some pro golfers sternly questioned their instructors. The reason for the uproar was because Charles Boswell was blind.

In November of 1944, Boswell boarded a tank to slip through closing German lines and get supplies for his troops. On the way back, the tank he was in was hit by a shell. As Boswell was attempting to crawl out of the tank, the Germans hit it with another shell. The last thing Boswell saw was a brilliant flash of light as the gas tank was blown up. At 29 years of age, Boswell, a husky 210 pound ex-halfback from the University of Alabama was now a blind war veteran.

Discouraged and depressed while recovering back home at Valley Forge Hospital in Pennsylvania, Boswell was approached by Cpl. Kenny Gleason, a golf pro and hospital staff member. Gleason suggested they go out and play golf. Bemused by the invitation, Boswell decided to go. Gleason handed him a 2 wood. He lined up Boswell and the face of Boswell's club with the ball and told him to hit it.

Boswell had maybe hit three balls in his entire life so when his club-head successfully hit the ball, he was startled. He wanted to know where it had gone. Gleason drily told him he had hit it 180 yards straight down the fairway. Boswell was hooked.

With a caddie or a companion to help line up his shots, Boswell was able to make it around a golf course. Within a short space of time, he was bombing 290 yard drives straight down the fairway and manipulating balls over sand traps and tree roots better than any player with sight.

Boswell's frequent assistant was his cousin, Dick Cox. Boswell would play in pitch darkness after Cox got off work and shoot 85 or 90 for 18 holes.

Some speculated that Boswell was able to play as well as he did because he took the same swing with every club. Also, Cox always gave Boswell exact yardage, which increased the preciseness of his shots.

Boswell, however, considered putts the easiest of shots, claiming that he could "feel" the distance.

Other golfers on the course who didn't know Boswell never suspected he was blind because of how well he played. For the tough determined Boswell, that was just the way he wanted it.

So when the instructor told me I had to keep my eye on the ball, I thought of Charles Boswell. But I wasn't about to dismiss her recommendation. I decided to listen to her. She was the instructor after all. She said there was no reason to "kill it." The club loft takes care of the ball. "Trust the club." Over the course of hitting a hundred balls, she was able to get me to hit a few decent shots. I was exhausted. Golf didn't seem like much fun on the range.

When I got back home, I told Joe the lesson had gone well. "When can we play?"

"One lesson and you think you can go golfing?" He shook his head and walked away.

My next lesson was two days later. This time the instructor put her hand on the top of my head to keep it still. I had terrible form. My left knee collapsed in, my head went in all directions and I was very hands-y with my shots. The only good thing was that I could tee up a ball fast.

When I hit two decent shots back to back, I felt this surge of confidence. I was eager for more. My lesson was over, but I kept hitting balls as my instructor moved on to her next student. Fatigue soon set in but I still began to bash balls, not realizing that I was integrating poor form into my reps. Hitting poor shots is not doing anything but creating a poor golf swing.

Early on, I believed that my swing was all my own. I was not trying to emulate any golfer, however, Joe loaded up our DVD player with numerous instruction videos for me to watch on how a swing should look. Charles Howell III was one of the swings used to teach proper form and try as I might, I could not remotely emulate his swing. I was a forty year old woman, not a twenty-something male athlete!

The teaching materials only served to increase my anxiety about golf. I wanted golf to be fun, but instead, it was coming across as an assault of information. Do this, don't do that, remember this, remember that. My head was filled with thoughts and it only made me squeeze the club tighter and stand paralyzed over the ball.

On the practice range, I looked around. There were no other females. I saw men standing over the ball for at least 20 seconds as if thinking of all the things to do and not to do before a shot. It took them forever to hit the ball and then the shot was still poorly executed. Golf was becoming a turn-off.

I reluctantly attended my third lesson, but it went poorly and I was not able to hit one ball off the ground or even off a tee. It just felt like work – sweaty work. I wanted to feel free and have fun, not work. The teacher recommended I try playing a local Par 3 course named Casserly. I had "beaten" Joe at that Par 3 course in

Stanley Park in Vancouver, so maybe Casserly would be fun.

Well-maintained and in an attractive setting, I took on Casserly with all the seriousness of a major championship. In the morning, I spent a few hours mentally preparing myself, cleaning my clubs and making sure my golf bag was in order. I wore slacks, a moisture wicking shirt and a vest. Proper golf shoes covered my feet. I looked like a golfer and that gave me confidence. Once I got to the course, however, all that mental confidence was gone. I sat in my vehicle a jumble of nerves. The parking lot was full. All these people would see how truly awful at golf I was! I took a few deep breaths and wobbled my way into the little golf shop. The attendant wanted to know what I wanted.

"I.. I want to play golf." Duh. Why else would I be there? He stared at me with a blank look on his face. I started to wonder if there was another reason I would be there.

He scrutinized me. "Nine?"

"I…?"

"Nine or eighteen?"

I shook my head. I didn't know what he was talking about.

"Are you playing nine or eighteen holes?"

"Oh, I think I should try nine first."

He shook his head. "That will be five dollars."

I took out my neatly folded five dollar bill and handed it to him.

"Do you need a scorecard?"

"Uh…?"

He pursed his lips and pushed a white card at me. "Here's a scorecard and a pencil. You write down how many shots it takes you to hit on each hole."

"Oh." I looked at the card. All the numbers on it seemed daunting. It was the first time I had ever seen a scorecard. I had no clue how to read it, but after studying it for a few minutes I understood.

Joe had told me to get a walking cart so I would not have to carry my bag, so I asked the attendant for one. Again, he scrutinized me. It would be an additional two dollars.

I went out to a shack near the "pro" shop and chose a cart. I fumbled with it, trying to figure out how to secure my bag. There was no strap, so I held my bag with one hand as I made my way over to the first tee. There were several players lined up and I felt my nerves spike.

The attendant came out of the shop and told me that it was a *push* cart - I was pulling the cart behind me, slamming it into my ankles and weaving along the grass. Embarrassed, I hurriedly adjusted to a pushing position.

"And your scorecard is upside down," he added, disappearing back inside the shop.

I was mortified. Being out there was a big deal to me and I took the embarrassment hard. There was no one to guide me through those simple steps. Like most situations in my life, I learned things by fumbling my way through it.

The course was busy and I let a bunch of players through so no one would have to see me tee off. The attendant stood in the doorway leaning against the frame, watching. When I finally got the guts to play, I dismissed the green mat that was there to hit shots from and instead teed up the ball in the ground and took out my driver. I had not hit from a mat before. I only knew how to swing at shots that were on the grass or on a tee.

"No! No!" the attendant yelled.

I was confused and rattled. He strolled over, shaking his head. He said the first hole was merely 105 yards.

There is no way I would need a driver on that hole. I felt foolish and asked him what I should hit. He said whatever club I hit at that distance. I had no clue. I had never read or been told to learn how far I hit each club and at this point, I hit most clubs the same distance except for my driver. So I guessed it was a 5-iron that would get me to the green. I swiped at the ball and it rolled along the ground half-way to the green.

The attendant shook his head. "It's going to be a long day."

On I went, trying to remember what my instructor had told me. Keep my head down. Don't lift up my left heel. Don't try to kill it. I made my way around the course in much the same fashion: teeing off with a shank or hook, pop-up or duffed shot, bounding my second, third or fourth shot short of or over the green and three putting or worse. With each lousy shot, I felt demoralized. There were so many people playing, I had to wait and when it was finally time to hit, I shriveled under their watchful eyes hitting one bad shot after another.

"I'm just learning. This is my first time," I said to everyone I met, apologetic.

I would see them take a swing and land the ball right near the hole. My shoulders slumped with dismay, knowing it took me several shots to get to the green.

I had such high hopes based on my memory of Stanley Park in Vancouver, but this outing confirmed I could not play golf; so much for all those dreams and "visions" and that strong desire. I couldn't take on a simple Par 3 course. What a joke!

I went home and felt sorry for myself for the next few weeks. I didn't want to go back to the instructor. She didn't seem that into it and I felt uninspired by her instruction. I was too embarrassed to return to Casserly and I didn't even want to watch golf. How could I want something so badly and yet perform so poorly? It made no sense to me.

Wintertime came on and I finally decided to return to the range, but first, I decided to keep things simple. Casting aside all those thoughts that would bombard my mind when I set up over a ball, I kept my golf swing to four simple steps: head down, eye on ball, club back and through. The ball did not go very far, but I was making contact consistently like never before. The more shots I was able to hit well, the more my confidence grew and that allowed me to feel freer and more willing to take some risks. Incrementally, I began to add more of the proper fundamentals to my swing, but I struggled with trying to keep my left arm straight. It always bowed or collapsed, but I kept returning to the range, thinking that this was my only way of playing golf for the foreseeable future so I better enjoy it.

Then one day Joe said, "Let's go play golf."

*

Nearly forty years after having those "visions", January 24, 2007 was my first official round of golf. Perhaps the dead of winter was not the best time to go even if it was California wintertime. I bundled up for 48 degree weather, but I was burning with excitement. On the short drive over to the course, I tried to conjure up in my brain all those lessons I had read or watched on video or DVD, but they had never really taken hold because I didn't have any real sense of how to play the game. My head was swirling with a number of thoughts. Would I make a fool of myself like I had at Casserly? Would someone yell at me to get off the course? Would Joe lose his patience and this be the one and only time we would golf together? Was I simply too old to start playing golf?

Tom Watson said that the younger you learn how to play golf, generally, the better you will play. When he was about 8 years old, he was on a family trip travelling by car in Colorado. His father made an impromptu stop at a public course in the Rocky Mountains. When Tom and his father went to check in, the man behind the counter said that Tom could not play unless he could hit his ball over a creek that was about 60 yards from the first tee. Tom's father agreed and they all went out to the first tee. There, Tom loosened up with a few practice swings, teed up the ball and hit it over the creek about 125 yards right onto the fairway. The attendant said that Tom would be allowed to play.

By learning golf at an early age, Tom not only impressed the golf shop attendant with his form at the age of 8, he was on track to become one of the greatest golfers in the history of the game.

When we are young, the body is supple and for most, the mind is like a sponge, absorbing information. Because golf is a sport that can be enjoyed for an entire life – as long as one is healthy – to start early on with the fundamentals meant more time to enjoy the game and be better at it; at least for the majority of players.

Learning the proper grip and the proper stance as early as possible was Watson's recommendation. With the proper stance you can maintain balance. With the proper grip, you can keep control of the club. Once you know how to do that, you can set up to a ball and let it rip. Even if you whiff it or top it or send it so far left you can't find it, it's okay. By babying a ball in order to make it go straight, you can never hit it with any power. The same firmness applied to putting. Hitting the ball firm and with confidence was how to sink putts. Hitting as few bad shots as possible was how to shoot a great round of golf because bad shots are a guarantee.

Nerves were normal, Watson said, but over time they dissipate as you gain confidence in what you are doing. One attack-of-the-nerves' moments happened early on when he was fifteen years old. Watson was the city match-play champion and selected to play in a charity exhibition with none other than Arnold Palmer. But as nervous as Watson was, he hit his best drive ever, about 260 yards. Palmer did a double take. Palmer then stepped up and ripped his drive past Watson's ball. Later in the round when Watson holed a 25-foot putt for birdie, Palmer did another double take. Watson shot 74 that day to Palmer's 68. After that match, Watson realized that if he could play golf with Arnold Palmer, he could play with anybody. That helped Watson put playing the game of golf into perspective.

When Palmer was in his 50s and struggling to keep up with the younger players, he was asked if that bothered him. "Playing badly is still better than not playing at all," Palmer replied.

The point was to keep playing for the enjoyment and for the challenge because no matter how great a round you shot, not every single shot would be perfect. Watson emphasized that no matter how much golf you play, you will never master the game. Despite all of his success, there were days when he would go out and just not be able to swing well. Sooner or later, his sweet swing came back, but he understood it would go away again. For him, that was part of the joy of the game. The challenge of it, the elusiveness of it and the fact that you can always go back and try again.

It was on the drive over to the golf course that I thought about all of these things. Would my swing, such as it was, be there on my first official day of golf?

CHAPTER ELEVEN

The Fade

Spring Hills Golf Club is a comfortable course in a bucolic setting and was a good place for my first round of golf. It was more dry grass than lush fairways and greens, but it was a good course for a beginner. Joe called it a "cow pasture." Well, I had read all about people learning to play golf in cow pastures and they had done just fine.

Like Casserly, I had to learn a lot of little things I had not even considered like getting the golf cart, knowing how to arrange the golf cart, being quiet on the tee box, how to wash my golf balls, how to stay behind the tee boxes when teeing it up, not standing in my partner's peripheral view and most all, breathing and relaxing. That was the most difficult thing to remember.

My heart was pounding on the first tee while I awaited Joe's drive. The course was not crowded. We were a twosome, but there were people milling around the nearby parking lot. I imagined everyone was staring at us. I was overcome with nerves. Joe set up and fired his drive, a sweet bomb right down the middle of the fairway. My legs felt like noodles as I walked to the forward tee. I delicately put the tee in the ground and placed the ball on top of the tee. It wobbled off. I re-teed it and then bumped it with my driver, knocking the ball off. Once more I teed up the ball and backed away slowly, trying to focus. I sucked large amounts of air but only succeeded in hyperventilating. I fidgeted back and forth.

"Come on!" Joe yelled.

I squeezed the life out of the grip on my driver. Somewhere in my head, I heard Nick Faldo say, "Lovely hands." I had heard him say that phrase so many times during a golf telecast and it helped me relax my hands yet have a steady grip. I took the club back slowly and then fired. I launched it in the air but hooked it. The ball bounded across the road, never to be seen again.

"Just relax and tee it up again," Joe said.

Same result.

"Damn it," I yelled. "It's this stupid left off-set driver you bought me."

"Yeah, that's it," Joe replied, shaking his head. "Come on let's go. You only get one mulligan off the tee."

"What's a mulligan?" I asked as we drove about 150 yards.

"Two drive attempts off the first tee."

Knowing that helped me relax. He then told me to tee up the ball in the fairway. The hole has an exaggerated dogleg right (almost like a V-shape), so I couldn't see the green or even understand where I was hitting it. With determination, I jammed the tee in the ground and placed my bright pink Precept ball on the tip. I tried hitting driver once more. I hit the ground first and then managed to shank the ball about 30 yards where it got stuck up on a steep hillside.

By now, a twosome had arrived at the first tee and were standing with their hands on their hips. I was beginning to feel the pressure to get a move on.

"I can't play this game!" I wailed.

"Oh, come on, just relax," Joe said, then expertly hit his ball to a great spot to approach the green.

I soon learned not to whine loudly about my shot when someone else was trying to focus on their game. I also learned to not clang my clubs when someone was hitting a shot. Most of all, Joe said to keep calm, no matter what. That was one of the more difficult tenets in golf to remember. I hurriedly hacked away at the ball, skittering it along the ground until I finally made it onto the front edge of the green in 12 shots. Joe was patiently waiting to putt for birdie from about 10 feet.

After four putts, I made it into the hole. Joe ended up making par. He wasn't exactly having a good time waiting around for me, but he did not express his discontent.

The second hole was tricky. A 427 yard Par 4 with a tiny creek that cuts off the fairway as you approach the green. It was 340 yards for me. I confidently teed it up and launched a 100 yard drive with my Cobra driver right into the center of the fairway. Now that was progress.

Joe expertly hit a drive 280 yards and then waited – patiently – as I skulled the ball on the ground for my next four shots before finally hitting it into the creek. Frustrated and embarrassed, I picked it out of the creek as Joe hit his second shot onto the green. I placed my ball on the ground and then proceeded to hit my next shot right back into the creek.

"I quit! These stupid clubs are not working properly!"

"Just relax. You're trying too hard."

My head was spinning. My brain was bombarded with thoughts and I couldn't remember one thing about just doing a very simple golf swing. I sat in the golf cart struggling to clear my mind.

No one can go out and play with a completely empty mind; thoughts always crop up warned Sam Snead. But he had a suggestion; a way in which to bend the mind that would help. He believed in having a friendly attitude toward the golf ball. Thinking it was to blame for your missed shot was not the way to go. And if you did have the kind of imagination that made you think your ball was the enemy, you could also imagine the ball to be your friend. Snead even recommended smiling at the ball on your down-stroke. Treating the ball well, as a friend, eased the tension within yourself and caused you to relax. It was a great metaphor for life. Are you going to look at challenges in a friendly manner, or have a tense angry attitude? The choice was up to you. You may win a battle by being angry (Snead admitted it stoked his fire for a while), but the friendly way always came out on top.

Snead further encouraged simple mind games when on the course. He recommended that golfers imagine that par on most holes is one stroke more than it really is so that the golfer could stay within himself and not try to bash the ball, which would lead to bungled shots. In doing this, he found that most golfers were actually able to subtract shots rather than add shots to their score.

Snead realized that everyone has a different capacity for concentration, imagination and mental toughness. He called Ben Hogan "stone face" for his tense manner and Tommy Bolt "Thunder" because he was always storming around and breaking things. Once, during a tournament, Bolt got so angry that he tried to break his club over his knee, but it just bent around his leg like a pretzel and he had to take his shoe off before he could wriggle the club off his leg. Rage was not the way to play golf.

Figuring out how to cast aside bad thoughts and clear your mind and use that to better your golf game was a key component to successful play. Despite touting this, Snead knew we all fell victim to over-thinking and frustration. He said steam would come out of his ears over a bad shot until he remembered to sweet-talk the ball. Even if he found his ball in an impossible lie, he would say, "Hey you beautiful little white thing! What are you doing down in that hole?"

Snead also recognized everyone's need to vent and that given the complex emotions of human beings, there was no way possible to stay even-minded and steady on a golf course every single time out, but his recommendations were given as a way for players to get back on track, to never lose sight of the fact that the game was offering an opportunity for enjoyment not self-flagellation.

For players like Hogan and Bolt, Snead could see a sharp contrast in their mental approach to the game. But Snead thought that Hogan wasn't as tough as he appeared to be on the course. After sharing a room with Hogan one night when on the road, Snead couldn't sleep a wink. Hogan was loudly grinding his teeth all night long. One way or another, we all have to vent.

Part of Snead's reflections on the mental aspects of the game came from what happened on the 18th hole in the final round of the 1947 US Open at St. Louis Country Club, Ladue, Missouri. He was playing with Lew Worsham and they were tied on the last hole. They both had a short putt about the same distance. Snead felt great; none of the tournament pressure was getting to him. He was about to make a lovely roll right into the hole when Worsham spoke up, claiming to be away and called for a measurement. As they waited for the officials to bring in the tape measure, Snead's temperature was rising. He was so upset that when it was determined that he was in fact away and could go ahead and putt, he couldn't even see the ball through his fury. There was only a loud clanging in his head and he could barely breathe. Snead yipped the 30-inch putt and lost the US Open. Was Worsham to blame for what was likely a parlor trick or was Snead to blame for his inability to control his emotions? Snead blamed himself.

Putting required 100 percent mental focus, Snead felt. It was what determined winning from losing. Unfortunately, short putts caused him the most stress. Being able to concentrate over a putt was the key. Concentration saps the energy, but so does a cluttered mind. Simple thoughts equaled simple strokes.

I had to clear my thoughts and I had to improve my attitude to get that simple swing I had worked out on the range. I picked up my ball, smiled at it and said, "Hello." I was determined to start fresh.

The third hole had a creek running along the entire right side of it and I found it all right, but this time with a cheery attitude. Unfortunately, Joe also found the creek and he was steaming mad.

By the time I got to the green, I was exhausted, having skulled, topped or barely launched 15 shots. I didn't take long over shots, so I wasn't taking up a whole lot of time to delay the twosome behind us but still, my game stunk! I felt I had been delusional all along. Me, golf? Obviously not. I tried to smile but instead stewed in frustration on the ride to the next hole.

The fourth hole was a 341 yard Par 4 that played 325 yards for me. Unfortunately that darn creek also ran all along the right side of this fairway and Joe found it as soon as he launched his tee shot. I kept fixating on the fact that my ball would also end up in the creek so I lined up as far left as possible. Shockingly, I launched my drive 125 yards tracking down the left side, but safely in play. It felt great! I was so full of myself I ran over to my ball. I lined up over my next shot for several seconds, knowing that if I just did what I did on the tee box, I could get a par – or even better, a birdie. Yup, I was going to be on the green in two. Instead, I scuttled it 50 yards to the right. My heart sank.

Joe drove the cart over to his ball. We watched it be-bopping along down the flowing creek. Joe had to make a decision where to drop his ball. I was determined to hit my next shot onto the green so I leaped out of the cart and set up over my ball.

"Ahem," he cleared his throat. "It's rude to hit out of turn."

"Oh," I said disappointed. I was so eager to hit my ball. I just knew this time I would land it on the green. I moved out of his line, silently urging him to quickly hit his shot so I could go after mine.

Joe took a lateral drop and hit his ball into the rough surrounding the green. He flung the club in anger.

"Hit your damn shot!" he yelled.

I was startled by his behavior but eager to take on my shot. I took out a pitching wedge, stepped up to the ball, took the stance of a player I had seen on television, reminded myself to stay down and struck a gorgeous pitch right onto the green about ten feet from the hole. *Somebody stop me!*

I marched up with confidence, thinking, "Oh, yeah, I've got you now hole."

I fidgeted around with impatience, waiting for Joe to chip *his damn shot* onto the green. He backed off three times and I went ahead to study my putt.

"I'm chipping here," he remarked, his voice high-pitched with stress.

"You're taking forever."

"I'm entitled to take my time."

I backed off and sulked until finally he flubbed his chip barely onto the green.

"See what you made me do!"

I felt bad, but part of me also didn't care. I had a putt for par and I was going to tell everyone in the clubhouse how I got a par on my first time out (as if anyone would care).

My mouth was dry. My neck was tense. My arms even more tense. I lined up over my putt. *I've got you now sucker.* I gave it a blast. I couldn't wait to witness it drop into the hole and I instantly turned and watched it, ready to give that roaring Tiger fist pump. I pulled it ten feet past the hole. Two more putts later, I drained it. So much for that par. My heart sank. I had felt so *high* thinking about sinking my par putt and now I was deflated. Golf was not supposed to make me feel this way, right?

I decided I would make it happen on the 5th hole, a 348 Par 4 that was a mere 275 yards for me. Oh yeah, this hole was mine. I then proceeded to "hit" my tee shot a mere 30 yards into the creek running all along the left side of the fairway. That damn creek was following me!

"Take a drop!" Joe yelled.

Determined and gripping my driver firmly so that I could communicate to it what I wanted it to do, I hit a "gorgeous" tee shot (120 yards) right back into the drink.

"Take a lateral when we get down there," Joe said, resigned to an agonizing round of golf.

Eight shots later, I made it to the hole. I simply could not figure out the concept of hitting down on the ball to make it go up in the air. My left knee collapsed as did my left arm and I dipped my right shoulder. It was hideous form. Sure, on the range where I teed up every ball, I was able to launch a few shots, but here on this, this *cow pasture* how was I supposed to launch it? I imagined that if I was playing a high class course like Pebble Beach I would launch it *no problem.*

The one positive on that hole was that I did drain a six-foot putt. You celebrate the good stuff when you can because they are few and far between when first starting out in the game.

The par 5 452 yard 6th hole looked intimidating. By now, I felt deflated, tired, disinterested even. What a stupid set of clubs I had. They didn't do what I wanted them to do. Maybe if I had Tiger's clubs I would be launching it *no problem.*

My stunning 160 yard drive right down the middle of the fairway (avoiding that creek that was chasing me) surprised me. It was such a great feeling. Why were those feelings so infrequent?

Joe had driven it way past me to where the hole doglegs right. I took my 3 wood and with all the confidence I had gained from my drive, proceeded to hit the ball, knowing I would get my second shot near the green. I dribbled it 10 yards.

"This stupid club!"

"You topped the ball," Joe said.

"Because of the club!"

Joe rolled his eyes and shook his head, trying to focus on his own shot. He placed it expertly onto the green a few feet from the hole. Jealousy coursed through me. I wanted to do that.

Five shots later I made it into the hole. I was so embarrassed by my game that I felt extremely nervous when a twosome came up behind us. I didn't want them to see how badly I played. Maybe they would yell at me that I was holding up their game. Maybe they would call the club house and I would be physically removed from the course.

I sat out the 7th and 8th, a difficult Par 4, 400 yard uphill hole. Perhaps I should have played the 8th given that it was not a water hole, but I couldn't get my thoughts together and I thought it would help us speed up play so the twosome behind us would not be on top of us.

We then headed to the Par 3 9th hole, an elevated tee to a green with that creek running in front of it. I duffed my tee shot right into the water. *That does it! I can't play golf!* I walked to the cart and sat there fuming. I was embarrassed, ashamed, angry and deflated all at once. Joe had placed his tee shot nicely a few feet from the pin and would drain his putt for a birdie.

My conviction to master my game surged as I lifted my ball out of the water and took a lateral. I had dreams of pitching the ball right onto the green. *I can do this.* I hurriedly grabbed my 60 degree wedge and proceeded to blade my shot right across the green, nearly hitting Joe.

"You're supposed to yell fore!" he barked.

"I thought that was just for strangers, not for you. I thought you were supposed to be watching my ball!"

His shoulders slumped in exasperation. The last thing he wanted to do was have a couple's argument on a golf course. When he sank his birdie putt, I congratulated him. I figured it was the right thing to do even if I felt envious.

As we drove to the tenth tee, Joe asked me if I wanted to continue playing.

"Of course! Why wouldn't I?"

"Because it doesn't look like you are having any fun."

"But I sank that last putt for a quadruple bogey."

"Exactly."

I shrunk down in the cart. Sinking the putt, *eventually,* was not really something to celebrate. Hitting good shots, shot by shot was really what I needed to do.

"I can do it. Let's go."

The tenth hole was an uphill 163 yard par 3. I had 143 yards from my tee with water on the right. All I

could think about was, "Don't hit it in the water!" Sure
enough, I hit it in the water.

Joe struggled too, hitting the ball way left and yelled
that he couldn't concentrate because of all the noise
from the driving range that was near the tenth tee. Well,
we all have our excuses.

Joe was able to get up and down for a bogey but I
struggled with trying to pitch up the hill to the green.
First, I was too timid and decelerated on my shot. Then,
I was too bold and bladed it over the green. Then I was
timid again and nudged it into the rough. Ugh, the
frustration!!

It was obvious to me now how skilled the pros are
and how *laughable* it was to think I could make my way
around a course in a skillful fashion my first time out.

I began to wish the round was over as we headed to
the 468 Par 5 11th hole. From my tee, I had 430 yards to
go, but it may as well have been 1,000 yards. Hitting the
ball barely to the right would result in the tee shot
landing in long grass. At least there wasn't water on this
hole. The green was dogleg left and Joe found it in
three. I was still whacking my ball down the fairway like
a hockey puck (a poorly struck hockey puck).
Sometimes I was able to launch the ball maybe three feet
off the ground, but mostly I just rolled it along the
fairway.

"Maybe this is how I should play golf," I said as I got
into the cart. "I can just roll it on the ground."

"Then you're not playing golf," Joe replied. Happy
that he was putting for birdie, he was more encouraging.
"Just keep your eye on the ball and hit down on it."

I got a 15 on that hole while Joe scored his birdie. He
was grinning from ear to ear.

As I went to the next tee, a 338 Par 4 (315 yards for
me) my eyes were full of tears. The course was exposing

me for who I was: just a dreamer. I had no right to be out there. It was an insult to the course – to courses everywhere to "play" like this. I stepped up to the ball and hit a gorgeous 180 yard tee shot right down the fairway. My jaw dropped. I had just given up. How did that happen?

Over my next shot, I kept saying to myself *hit down on the ball, hit down on the ball.* I bashed the ball right on top of its head and it hopped and skipped a few yards. "I can't do this!" I wailed.

"Hit behind the ball, not on top of it!"

"Well, you didn't say that!"

"Jeeeeeez…"

The twosome behind us were now on top of us. "Go on through," Joe yelled.

The guys waved while we moved off to the side of the fairway.

"What's going on?" I demanded.

"When you are a slow player, you let others through."

"But… but then we will have to wait for them."

"I seriously doubt that."

I watched (impatiently) as one guy flailed at his ball and shanked it while his partner drove his ball way left.

"Maybe it wasn't such a good idea," Joe commented and we moved back to our balls.

This time, I focused on the shot and looked behind the ball. I used a 4 hybrid (to make it go far and all) and made good contact, hitting it about 120 yards but it went left (which makes the ball go further). I kept closing the club-face as I came down and rolling my wrists to the left.

I watched the twosome we had let through finish out on the green. Three shots later, I sunk the putt for bogie. I was elated. That was just one shot off par! Joe was glad I was happy.

As the round continued, fatigue set in my legs and I had an impossible time staying down over the ball. My mental focus was drifting as well. What would we have for dinner? Were the dogs okay? I wonder why I feel so sweaty? When can we golf again?

Joe's game declined as we neared the end of the round. At one point, I found myself in the rough around the green on the 15th hole. I took my 60 degree wedge and chipped it within a foot of the hole. I was stoked but Joe yelled at me that I had used poor technique by stabbing at the ball. I was confused. Why was he so angry? I had put it within a foot of the hole. Wasn't that the point; to get it as close as possible? I realized then that he had just triple bogeyed the hole and was lashing out at me.

We drove home in silence after the round.

"You did good," Joe said, surprising me.

"I stunk!"

"It took me years to learn how to play golf."

"But I've *waited* years to play golf."

"Then you have to practice every day if you want to get better faster."

I wanted to get back out there and play again but I felt I simply could not do it. A couple of days later I returned to the practice range, determined to work on my shots. The tee shots were fine, but rarely went more than 150 yards. My irons were inconsistent. The woods were non-existent and I launched maybe 50 percent of the balls with my wedges.

Next to me on the range, a young woman was hitting balls. She drilled them expertly, launched them loftily and wedged them perfectly. I took note of her clubs: A Ping Driver and Touredge irons and wedges. That must be the reason she was hitting her shots so well.

I began to blame the clubs I had for my poor shot-making and I bought myself a new Ping driver and a set of Tour Edge irons and wedges. Wow, was I excited when they arrived. I couldn't wait to get out there and attack the course. I just knew I would hit the ball like that girl did on the practice range.

I was wrong.

CHAPTER TWELVE

Pin Hunting

More than 150 rounds of golf would follow over the next year. I was sinking an occasional birdie and racking up a few pars. Slowly, I was lowering my handicap. I had some good shots, but I still had numerous hooks and slices.

Gene Sarazen believed that a poor grip is what contributed to hooks and slices. If the left hand is too far over on the shaft, the right hand is then too far under the shaft. The grip results in a very flat swing. Addressing the ball with this improper grip often results in your hands working their way back into the position they should have been in when you addressed the ball. Unfortunately, then it is too late because the club-face is closed. If you are gripping the club properly, you can then swing freely.

Once a proper grip is established, watching the club-head go back was the next important step. In Sarazen's opinion, almost everyone takes the club back too much on the inside. The problem with this is the club will come down on the outside, cutting across the ball. The key was not to develop many years of improper gripping and takeaway or correcting the resulting problems would be very difficult.

It had taken me forty years to get here and I didn't want to develop bad habits that would further delay my enjoyment, but in truth, I had amassed a number of bad habits. Ultimately, Sarazen, like Tom Watson, believed that once you could establish a good grip and stance, experience would be the best teacher.

I returned to reading Ben Hogan's *Five Lessons* and studied it now with a different eye because I had the benefit of actually having some experience on the course. The instruction in the book began to make more sense to me. I applied the methods on the practice range and on the course. My game started to improve. Some shots were beautiful, like miracles. Other shots were as abysmal as ever. But the hunger and enjoyment were there because the good shots were enough to keep me going. After each round, even though I was exhausted I wanted to start off again at the first tee.

My desire for golf was greater than anything. I couldn't wait to leave the house to get to the range or the course, but my anxiety issues had not entirely disappeared. Most of the courses we played paired us with other twosomes and when this happened, I felt self-conscious and it affected my game. I thought the people we were paired with would have their rounds affected by my sometimes 12 shots to the green. I was so worked up with this belief that it often took me five or six holes to settle down and when I did, I shocked our playing partners with my suddenly well-struck drives right down the middle of the fairway or some amazing chips around the green. It felt good when other players complimented my shots and were supportive. Pairings, however, were not always a positive experience.

There were plenty of men who could have done without my presence. I was impeding their ability to truly relax by swearing, passing gas and acting like cavemen. Others acted like I didn't even exist. Whenever Joe would hit his drive, they would follow with their drives and then I would step onto the forward tee, but they would already be heading down the fairway to their balls before I had even teed off. If they did wait, some would chat up a storm or make so much noise that I was distracted.

This behavior was not limited to the tee box. Often when Joe was putting, the male playing partners were still and silent. When I was putting, they would talk, move around or make noise.

Even the placement of the forward tees by the golf course management seemed to be an after-thought. The men would drive off their tees while my "forward" tees were a mere two or three yards in front of the men's tees. I had an impossible time getting to a Par 4 in two or a Par 5 in three.

Joe did find a course with a fair set-up on the forward tees. Note that I prefer to call them forward tees rather than women's tees. Too often players will not play the forward tees because they think they will embarrass themselves by going on the "women's tees" or the "junior's tees" and therefore play from a tee set back further. Jack Nicklaus has spoken on this issue before, insisting we call the forward tees just that, 'forward tees.' And by the way, Nicklaus said he now often plays from the forward tees. Are you going to call Nicklaus a lady? I don't think so.

The course that had a fair set-up off the forward tee boxes is San Juan Oaks in Hollister, California. A Freddy Couples' designed course, it not only has a sweet set-up for females, but it is smack dab in a quiet, natural setting where the most noise you will hear is a raptor flying overhead.

San Juan Oaks is also the course where Joe went to watch a Nationwide Tour Event. Joe was able to see talented golfers dissect this course like he and I never could. We then began to follow the Nationwide Tour which would later become the Web.Com Tour. We met golfers Joseph Bramlett, Zack Miller (who was paired with Hunter Mahan and Phil Mickelson on Sunday at the 2011 Pebble Beach Pro-Am), Julian Trudeau (runner up on the Golf Channel's 2011 Big Break) and Steve Friesen, who won the 2011 Price Cutter Charity Championship. It added a whole new enjoyment to golf, watching these players earn their way up through the ranks.

I paid close attention whenever we got to see a professional golfer play in person, believing that it would improve my game. Golf writer P. Beardsell Burn wrote a tongue-in-cheek article on the merits of actually being able to learn something as a member of the gallery:

"The play at any of the more important events of the golfing year is always full of interest to the onlookers. Those that make up the gallery see most of the game but had Sherlock Holmes been a golfer he probably would have said that the gallery sees but does not observe.

There are difficulties for the casual golfer who journeys many miles to the championships in the hope of picking up a secret or two. Even if every stroke in the game was seen from the first tee shot to the final putt it is difficult to say that the spectator is much the wiser. In the first place, there are hundreds of spectators and to get near enough to see how the trick is done is really difficult when a cavalry of marshals is yelling, "Get back please!" A position a few yards to the right or left of the player allows no chance of seeing the line to the hole as the player views it. Also, when in the crowd, it is impossible to gauge with much accuracy the strength of the wind that player has to contend with.

Suppose we do succeed in obtaining a point of vantage close to the player, what then? We are not much better off in learning anything because these eminent players do not spend much time over the actual playing of the stroke. A waggle or two, a glance towards the green in quite a casual sort of way, and almost before you have a chance to prevent the person behind you from pushing you into a bunker in his anxiety to see the shot, the thing is done.

There are, however, some lessons to be learned at these big golf events. The first thing, particularly on a Sunday, is probably the extreme seriousness of the players. There is none of that quick banter between the players that is such an enjoyable feature of the games on your own home course. They seem to realize that golf at a championship is a serious matter and indeed it is for one bad shot (even a moderately bad shot) will probably cost the perpetrator the hole or even a lot of money. The pro golfers take their time before each shot is played. It is easy to see that the player is calculating which is the better plan. Hit it, flop it or pitch and run it? Once they have decided, they play very quickly. In fact, the main idea when addressing the ball seems to be to get rid of it as soon as possible and that is by no means a bad plan.

The modern golf ball has caused most golfers to pay more attention to the cultivation of the pitch and run approach. The ball could bounce around in any manner. Brilliant approach shots are very pretty to watch. There is such a delicate grip of the club yet a firm and unyielding stroke. It seems simple enough, but it takes a lot of practice.

It is on and near the greens that the games are lost and won. The player who can lay long putts dead is usually the golfer to back as the eventual winner. Long putting is a ticklish business and it is not surprising to find the players spending quite a long time studying the green. The player walks alongside the line of his putt looking carefully at the ground, noting the dips and the little banks and the fast bits and the slow patches. He carefully removes anything likely to throw the ball off the line. He takes a look at the putt from hole to ball, walks slowly back and has a look from the ball to hole. He then sets up to his line and plays his stroke. It is with some satisfaction when we see the player badly miss a three foot putt as we do ourselves. And they do miss them. Often. We are just inclined to forget that they hole some ticklish six footers at other times – putts that we could never sink if we spent hours over the hole.

The good putters strike the ball with a very free blow and the clear sound of impact is always heard. The ball cannot be struck truly unless it is struck cleanly and freely.

Every good player possesses the power of recovery to some extent. Some players are never quite on the right line yet they manage to halve or win quite a number of holes. The player who reaches the green in a stroke less than his opponent does not automatically mean he is going to win the hole. Don't lament. Remember that the hole is never lost until it is won."

When we attended the Pebble Beach Pro-Am in 2011 I did make the assumption that watching the pros was going to give me insight into playing the game. What I discovered more than anything is how athletic the players are, how much they practice and just how well you have to play to be on the LPGA, Web.Com or PGA Tour.

The ability to earn a living by playing professional golf is not fully appreciated by the public because we don't understand all that is involved. Getting onto the tour is difficult but remaining on the tour is also a challenge.

In 1994, golfer Steve Brodie made it onto the PGA Tour through Q school. He had been playing golf professionally since 1986 and working his tail off on the mini tours, ultimately winning 15 events. But like most male pro golfers, the goal is to make it onto the PGA Tour and when he did, he had several top 25 finishes. It was also financially rewarding to Brodie. In one season, he doubled what he had made during three years on the Nike Tour (now known as the Web.Com Tour). Unfortunately, his 1994 finish in the money standings was not enough to secure his PGA Tour card for the next year. Brodie returned to the Nike Tour before making it back onto the PGA Tour.

At the age of 30, Brodie was golfing as often as possible. Just making enough money to cover travel expenses, let alone provide for a family of six (four children) was a constant challenge. When he did win "big" he would make multiple auto or housing payments in advance. He and his wife had to pursue other work or endorsements to supplement their income.

With a schedule that involved being gone up to ten months out of the year, it was a great sacrifice for everyone involved. The challenge and the competition as well as his love for the game kept his fire lit throughout his long playing career. Today, Steve is a teaching professional in Auburn, California.

So whenever you get a chance to watch these players at a Web.Com event, go – it's worth it. Watching skilled players live is a pleasure. You may not learn much for your own game but you just might be able to get close enough to say hello to a future superstar in the game.

One of the professionals who impacted my golf game but who I never got to see play live is Sir Nick Faldo. Faldo has a way of giving advice on the television broadcast that sinks into my brain. Joe could have told me the same thing but it didn't penetrate my cortex the way Faldo said it.

The advice and instruction of pro golfers from all generations continues to resonate with me today. Bobby Jones was generous with his time and golf knowledge. He even had a question and answer column on golf. One of the most frequently asked questions of Jones was how best to make the approach to a green. To play these shots consistently well, Jones advised, required more experience and judgment than anywhere else on the golf course. A drive was a drive and a second or third shot may be obvious as well, but when it came to chipping, it was rarely the same thing twice. Fast sloping greens demanded good judgment of where to land the ball. There were so many factors to consider – the slope, the speed, the putting surface, the roll of the ball from the lie, the loft of the club and the trajectory of its short flight. Players who rush their shots when they are near the green are doomed to failure or are hoping for a lucky break. Thoughtful time, study and practice had to be put into this aspect of the game.

Next to the short approach, putting was the other thing Jones felt caused players fits. Whether golfers are professional or not, each one seems to go through a period of believing they have discovered the "secret" to putting only to soon find themselves frustrated again.

A golfer has a better chance of perfecting his putter than any other club, Jones believed. The mechanics are simple and there is a greater latitude for individual expression and accommodation of physical differences. Jones believed in an individualized putting stroke after the basic mechanics were taught to a player.

Whenever he felt that his putting was off, Jones would go back to following the same set of rules he had established for himself. First, he would carefully select the line he wanted the ball to follow. Next, he would align the face of his putter exactly square to the line. Third, he would think of nothing else except hitting straight along that line.

Accurate striking of the ball is essential because once on the green, bad putting is what increases a player's handicap. Jones believed that most bad putts were indecisively struck. Indecision comes from confusion in the player's mind. No one can expect to hit the ball properly when they are uncertain about the correct line, break or speed. Flinching or jabbing the ball spoils the putt which leads to further indecision and insecurity on the next putt. Once the line has been selected, the next thing is to hit the ball with confidence. Whether the chosen line is right or wrong doesn't matter. Hitting the exact line that you selected is what is important. As you learn to read greens better, hitting your line is going to be vital to sinking the putt.

Jones liked to tell the story of the 1925 US Open play-off with Willie Macfarlane at Worcester Country Club in Worcester, Massachusetts. In the play-off, Willie had a lead of two strokes as they teed off on the 14th hole. Macfarlane hit a beautiful tee shot while Jones smothered his shot. His ball failed to get out of the rough and when he tried to use a "spoon" to reach the green, he sliced the shot badly into more rough a hundred yards from the flag. When Willie pitched his second shot fifteen feet from the hole, Jones' hopes evaporated. Already two down, he thought he would lose another one, possibly two. As he walked to his ball, he was thinking about dropping a shot(s) and felt ready to give up. He then pitched his shot onto the green and it rolled straight into the cup. Rattled, Willie missed his putt. In an instant, Jones had gained two shots instead of losing two. By the end of the play-off, both men were tied, having each shot a round of 75. Because ties are determined by 18-hole playoffs, the men had to go out again for another 18 holes. Macfarlane won the second eighteen-hole playoff by shooting a 72 to Jones' 73.

Even though Jones lost the US Open, he remembered that shot well because of the chance it gave him. He insisted that skill had nothing to do with his chip-in. A certain amount of luck was involved. He cautioned, however, that your opponent also has the same chance at catching a lucky break.

Pro golfer Johnny Revolta confessed that when it came to golf, he was lucky. The multiple tour winner and former PGA Champion at Twin Hills Golf & Country Club in Oklahoma City, Oklahoma said that people had a tendency just to make everything about golf harder than it needed to be.

Revolta graduated from caddie to pro during tough economic times. While as a caddie working the pro shop in Wisconsin, he shined clubs, made sure that players paid for the golf balls and kept an eye on the shop while the pro was out on the course. He snuck in golf practice about 60 yards from the golf shop so that if the pro showed up, he could run back inside and pretend to be working. It enabled him to fine tune his short game and he attributed that stolen practice in helping him win the PGA Championship. Still, he insisted that a good deal of his game had to do with luck.

Revolta grew up playing on a small course that was hacked out of a pine forest. The fairways weren't much bigger than a hiking trail but it forced Revolta to be accurate with his tee shots. He did bemoan the fact that he was playing in Wisconsin where there were no significant professional tournaments where he could see the great players of the game. However, there were several golf pros in the area who provided him instruction and who he could play against. He learned a lot just by watching them play or hearing them talk in the locker room about their game. Most of them wanted to play for money and it put pressure on the players during a time when money was scarce. Revolta began to rack up the cash. Still, he considered his success part luck.

Revolta revered Gene Sarazen since his miracle shot at The Masters but he referred to that shot as "luck" as well. What Revolta meant was that good breaks (luck) often comes to the good golfer. However, he did not think that luck was exclusive to good golfers. He believed that duffers also had the same percentage of luck available to them. By having the belief that luck was available to every golfer it took some of the pressure off. Pressure off led to better golf and those lucky breaks just start showing up. Therefore, it was Revolta's advice to golfers that when they head out to the golf course to understand that they are lucky before they even set foot on the first tee box. For one thing, you are out playing golf rather than bent over picking crops or plowing a field or working in a coal mine. So just in that case, you are lucky. Further, you are out in the fresh air, so why not try your hand at a bit of luck?

There is a legend of a man named Byng who seemed like luck was always on his side. His great ability consisted in the demolition of his opponents but there was always a large helping of luck involved. It is said that some people are born to greatness while others have greatness thrust upon them. Byng was a cross between the two. Byng's luck was regarded as an article of faith. People say that only "death and taxes are a guarantee" but so was Byng's luck.

Whenever Byng and a partner played, the partner knew not only what the result would be but what he would say to his friends about his lack of fight. He would attribute it all to Byng's luck – and also find room for an adjective describing that luck.

Sand bunkers were of no import to Byng. If he didn't jump them, he ran through them. He was rumored to have ricocheted out of a pond clean through an impenetrable gorse bush and hole a seventy yard approach.

Golf writer CJ Gilbert recalled an occasion where he was playing Byng in a close match:

> "At a critical hole, Byng sliced his brassie and the ball disappeared down a rabbit hole. It was as if the end of the world had come or the equator had lost its bearings by the way Byng reacted. The enormity of the possibility of Byng losing was also felt by his playing partners and the caddies. They approached the treacherous excavation with the sentiment that a villainous little rodent had stolen Byng's ball. Byng walked up to the other side of the bank and there, perched up a yard from the other end of the hole was the fugitive ball. His reputation was saved.
>
> Another time Byng drove wildly into dense hawthorn at least eight yards in diameter. Again the caddies stood aghast but his playing partner emitted an unpardonable sigh of relief – until they all saw that the intelligent ball had safely threaded

its way through the maze and awaited Byng safely and cheerily in the open.

There had to be an explanation, if only one could hit on it. Some said that Byng existed as a minor planet. When he got driven out of bounds and bunkered in the Milky Way he passed a few million years like a sort of astronomical dog, dodging neighboring planets. This theory, however, lacked confirmation. Others said Byng was a rubber plant; this received incidental support from the fact that with the advent of the rubbacor ball, Byng had suddenly developed his transcendent game. Others approached the subject from the psychological side and talked of mesmeric influence. Byng's eerie waggle, like a series of undulatory passes over the ball, gave support to that theory. Whatever the explanation, Byng never courted misfortune. He was just beastly steady.

To see Byng negotiate a foot putt was a sight for the gods. He viewed it from the ball to the hole and then went down on his knees and surveyed it from the hole to the ball. He could see in half a minute whether to allow half a blade of grass or one and a half blades of grass for deflection. Then, and only then, would he take up his position. His head sank down into his shoulders or his shoulders rose up and enveloped his head – one could never be quite sure which it would be. His club was deliberately – very deliberately – swayed backward and with mathematical precision down the ball went."

There was, however, a day of Byng's humiliation according to CJ Gilbert:

"The day was murky. Thunder was in the air. The birds had ceased their song and looked mournful and dejected. Around the clubhouse, men murmured in groups and there was a general atmosphere of a coming catastrophe. Inside, the treasurer was running his hand through what remained of his flowing locks trying vainly to balance the green fees while the cherry whisky stood un-tasted at his side. The Club's vice president looked around at the sullen members and inquired what had happened. Cups of tea were getting cold and the watercress was untouched. What did it all mean? After a period of unspeakable tension, the mystery came to a head. Byng had been seen emerging from the last green. His head was bent as slowly he wended his way towards the clubhouse in melancholy silence. His partner followed, bowed with a humiliation he had been powerless to avert. A dozen speculations arose but it was clear that none of them encompassed the full depth of the horror.

When at last Byng's playing partner spoke, it was with trembling emotion. Byng had got into a gorse bush and had lost his new Haskell ball. A thunderbolt or an earthquake would have been a welcome alternative to this catastrophe. Some were for winding up the club then and there but it was found that the bylaws stood in the way. Others were for selling their sticks and relinquishing the game forever. But not Byng. When the first anguish had passed, he simply went to his bag and took out the offending brassie. He then looked at his shoe. A smile lit up his features as he stalked out of the clubhouse."

The members subsequently found out that Byng had got the pro to file a sixty-fourth of an inch off the heel of his brassie and put another nail in the toe of his shoe. Then Byng drove six balls off the first tee and placid contentment illuminated his face. From that point on, Byng's luck stood firm and immutable.

My own luck was about to arrive soon enough.

CHAPTER THIRTEEN

Committing To The Shot

It was a new and bizarre thing feeling territorial about a golf course, but that is precisely what began to happen to us. We were playing a series of local courses open to the public. When summer came, play increased. Whenever we were out on the course and it was crowded, Joe and I both began to feel angry at all those *clowns* out there holding us up. People in front would dawdle, stand over a shot for more than 30 seconds or gab on the tee box before taking their shots. It was maddening. I wanted open tee boxes, open fairways and open greens. This was *my time*. These people all needed to *get lost*. I felt desperate to play, desperate to experience what I had been denied for 40 years. As my anger and sense of entitlement escalated, my golf game suffered. Anger is never good for golf.

My attitude soured and before we would even get to a course, I would complain, "Yeah, let's hope we can get all 18 holes in within six hours."

Joe could see that I was miserable and he didn't like waiting either, but he tried to remind me that everyone was out there to have a good time and this was an opportunity for me to enjoy being out of the house and to focus on my game. That was difficult. I found that I had to keep a rhythm going in order for me to maintain my focus. Waiting five, ten or fifteen minutes between each shot was not a good flow. My golf game just got worse. Then, Joe suggested we become members at a municipal golf course that had not one but two courses on site: Bayonet/Blackhorse in Seaside, California.

It was a half hour drive to Bayonet/Blackhorse, but I leaped at the chance of finally getting to play a course that might not be so crowded. Bay/Black has its fair share of play given that it is open to the public, but it did offer two courses that are spectacularly maintained. My anger began to dissipate and my game once again improved. On this set-up, I was able to make more par putts and when I sank a 60-foot downhill severely breaking to the right putt for birdie on Blackhorse's Par 4 3rd hole, the feeling was beyond belief. Joe had given me the read and when I looked at the green, a dim "path" lit up and I could see the track I needed to follow. I hit the putt just perfectly as Joe encouraged it along the way. When it plopped into the hole, I fell to my knees. I was overwhelmed. I had on a few occasions missed birdie putts on Par 3 holes, but to sink a birdie from that distance on a Par 4 was a rush.

We rarely played with other golfers on Bay/Black and that was enjoyable in the sense that I did not have to feel self-conscious or be distracted by rude partners. However, the summer months became loaded with tourists and the play slowed. Traffic to and from the course also became a nightmare and before long, it took more than an hour to go in one direction. We took a break from Bay/Black during the summer, but I underwent horrible withdrawals from golf. We played local courses whenever possible and just put up with the slow play. It was better than not playing at all.

Over time, I was slowly lowering my handicap and I was now about a 23 handicap. I was embarrassed to be shooting in the 90s but Joe said it took him decades to finally shoot in the 80s because he did not maintain a practice schedule.

It was a lot easier to break 100 than it was to break 90. Every commercial out there that claimed it would lower my handicap captured my attention. The ads are so convincing. There is always some guy proclaiming that he could not break 80 or 90 no matter how hard he practiced until he discovered one simple secret or product that would not require hours of practice. But no matter what product I bought (or fell for) it did not replace sound fundamentals and confidence/committing to shots. That is what always gave me the most success on the course over a new ball or new club or new teaching device.

Golf writer John Dengel wrote a piece many years ago saying that for fun golf, shooting in the 90s is a sensible goal because the average recreational golfer only plays once per week, but there seems to be a stigma of shooting in the 90s that is unfair. It takes the fun out of golf as these same once per week golfers pursue the goal of breaking 90. It's great to have that goal if you have the time and dedication to practice, but it also often requires repeatedly playing on one course until you know it like the back of your hand.

Dengel argued trying to break 90 fostered a type of phobia. Arriving at the course with dreams of breaking 90, most golfers leave the course having shot closer to 100. Instead of recognizing this self-imposed pressure, the golfer bemoans every instance where he felt the course treated him unfairly, saying that the score does not reflect his true ability. It becomes a challenge to not feel bad about yourself by the end of the round.

Rather than continue to believe that shooting in the 90s is only for hackers, Dengel suggested embracing the fact that there is nothing wrong with shooting 90 particularly if you are playing once per week. He imagined that you did have other things to do in life like work, pay your bills, feed yourself and your family. Little things like that.

Statistically he noted that ninety percent of recreational golfers score 90 or more. It is an honorable range. Remember when you first started? Weren't you shooting well over 100?

Golf does not have to be an endurance test. Go out there with an attitude to have fun. If you want to pursue breaking 90, 80 or 70, fine, but that's not most of us. Having a goal of shooting 90 is plausible, something many golfers can do and gain satisfaction from it.

Dismissing those extra shots and moving on with a renewed vigor to the next shot is the key to not holding on to the bad feelings that come with those extra shots. Many golf greats know they are going to make bad shots. It's how they move on that is important. Walter Hagen always knew he was going to have some hideous shots, but he erased them by making birdies. You always have a chance. A 90 plus golfer can even wipe out those double-bogeys with pars rather than allow himself to spiral out of control.

For those who don't get to play during the winter months, the expectation and anticipation built up over the cold season brings out an unrealistic goal by springtime. Winter somehow managed to blur those memories of bogeys in the previous golf season to becoming a scratch golf by springtime. By summer, the golfer discovers once again that he or she generally shoots in the 90s and feels bad for another year.

Unlike other sports, in golf the real opponent is you – it's not even the course (although we blame the course). It requires a tremendous amount of practice and maintaining concentration in order to play even on a recreational level. Only you can devote yourself to hours of practice, but most cannot with work and family obligations. So therefore, only you are to "blame."

Dengel outlined the evolution of the recreational golfer. At first, he/she is a wide-eyed newcomer, embarrassed to even take a divot. He/she hopes to score 120 maybe less and is grateful when that occurs. As time passes, the golfer then enters Phase Two. Parring a hole here and there is very satisfying despite those triple bogeys. Playing golf is still fun and exciting.

Phase Three, Dengel argued, is when the trouble begins because once a golfer feels the rush of a birdie expectation kicks in. Missed shots are a monumental disaster and cause for grumbling over the next few holes or even the rest of the round, annoying your playing partners who may be blissfully enjoying Phase Two. Then, the golfer enters in the insidious Phase Four where he/she believes if he/she could just string together all the good shots, well, he/she would be a great golfer, maybe even a pro! The golfer tosses and turns all night after a round, unable to sleep, reliving each and every botched shot.

Once you have entered Phase Four, you are doomed. You tell everyone about your tough breaks and say that you would have shot 86 if it had not been for that clown who left the rake sticking up out of the bunker or the foursome of old ladies who made you wait so long that you lost your rhythm.

Golf is pure torture to a perfectionist, Dengel noted. It will never be a game the recreational golfer or many pros for that matter can perfect. Instruction can help, but without pure devotion to practice, it is unrealistic to believe that you can subtract shots from your handicap. Further, some instruction is overly complicated. One authority on the subject breaks down the swing into 56 basic elements. For the some-time golfer, it is just not worth robbing yourself of the fun of golf by clogging your head with a bunch of useless information.

Dengel imagined that the philosopher Socrates would have approached golf in this manner:

1. The grip is the most important element in golf, so get a grip on yourself.

2. Except when hitting the ball, don't bother keeping your eye on it. Appreciate the trees for their natural beauty rather than look at them as hazards. Looking around at the sky, the clouds, the distant mountains, breathing in the air will make you feel good if you embrace the beauty that is being offered to you. When you feel good, relaxed, you play better.

3. Try to sink those super long putts, but once your ball leaves the club-face, don't fret. Just remain calm even if it ends up in a sand trap rather than in the cup (considering the odds and all of you actually being able to sink a super long putt).

4. Compete with realistic zest against your playing partner (who probably shoots in the 90s just like you do).

5. Be humble. You can't reach the green. Understand that. Take more club.

6. Remember that the hardest shot to hit in golf is a straight ball. Not even the pros can always hit a straight ball (and many never do).

7. Understand that you – only you – are responsible for the way you feel.

Once I began to understand this, my attitude improved and my game improved. Instead of trying to force it, my game flowed more naturally and I was able to concentrate over each shot and give it the full attention it "deserves". When we returned to playing at Bayonet/Blackhorse winter was fast approaching. For us, playing in 45 to 50 degree weather with 20 to 35 mph winds was better than not playing at all, but it also presents a challenge. Bundled up in Gortex, we battled strong winds and driving rain as we made our way around an empty course stiff from the cold and constantly trying to keep our gloves and grips dry. It did not help my handicap playing in rough weather, but I just felt happy and grateful to be out there playing golf.

Cold weather extends into spring in the Monterey Bay area and one cold day in April 2010, the wind was gusting up to 30 mph in the 50 degree weather. Playing Bayonet, the course had been a grind all day long. When we finally stepped up to the 170 yard Par 3 14th (118 yards for me) my luck was due.

The pin was in the front. From the tee box, I set up to go for the pin. Because of the strong wind in my face, I took my 4-hybrid and made sure my club-face was square to the pin. Relaxed, confident and focused, I took my club back and hit it squarely. The ball fought the wind, dropped onto the green and one hopped into the hole.

I was still looking at the ground from hitting my tee shot when Joe started jumping up and down yelling about my hole-in-one. I was in disbelief and then ecstatic.

Many say that an average golfer or even a poor golfer can get a hole-in-one – it is not exclusive to the skilled golfer. All you need is a bit of luck. Well, I did go for the pin. I did set up well. I did battle high winds and rain. I did hit a pure shot. So maybe my improved form coupled with a bit of luck gave me the highlight of my recreational golf career (so far).

CHAPTER FOURTEEN

The Short Game

Joe encouraged me to find a female partner to play golf with. I was resentful about this. *He* was my playing partner and that is all I needed. Soon, I realized that he needed guy time out on the course. I began to branch out and played alone or was paired with other golfers, male or female.

In truth, I was ignorant to the achievements of modern professional female golfers such as Nancy Lopez, Annika Sorenstam and Lorena Ochoa until I took the time to pay attention.

Ochoa was 11 years old when she sauntered up to pro Rafael Alarcon at the Guadalajara Country Club and asked him to help her with her game. He asked what her goal was and she replied that she wanted to be the best player in the world. Her career was relatively short, only 8 years, but she acquired 30 professional wins and claimed the number one world ranking.

Sörenstam's achievements are astounding. With 93 professional wins and multiple awards including multiple LPGA Player of the year awards and induction into the World Golf Hall of Fame there are few who can compare with her achievements. Being a successful golfer has nothing to do with gender. It is about passion for the game, hard work, determination and drive. No one should be discouraged from the game for any reason.

Joe suggested that I sign up for tournament play events because he believed it would make me a better golfer, but just the thought of it made me feel too much pressure. Instead, we began wagering against each other.

He gave me two strokes on Par 5 holes and one stroke on the rest. I beat him almost every time.

I am always committed to getting better. We live close to the beach, so I would take a wedge and practice my sand shots while nearby kids giggled at me. Also, I began to work on strengthening my grip that had been weakened over time by my excessive work on a computer keyboard. By this time, we had adopted two dogs. One was a large canine who required a strong grip while walking her because she lunged at squirrels, cats, birds – anything that moved quickly. Walking Large Canine up hills and through fields with only my left hand strengthened it tremendously. Soon, I began writing with my left hand, eating with my left hand and using it more and more so that it would be as adept as my right hand.

I thought all of this would translate to great play but the closely shaved fairways of Bayonet/Blackhorse and my tendency to sweep the ball caused me to have a difficult time consistently launching my fairway shots, particularly my woods. If I skulled or topped the ball, it would frustrate me more than any other bad shot. Hitting down on the ball, trusting the club-face to launch the ball without lifting up is easy to mentally understand but it proved to be a challenge for a very long time. I still have to remind myself to stay down and stay with the ball.

Bayonet/Blackhorse has a few hardpan areas under cypress trees, so it was the first time I was challenged to play off this type of surface on a regular basis. It took me a while, but it was one of the few situations that I was able to grasp and execute well. Initially, I would ground the ball at address but once I began to choke down on the grip and play the ball closer to my rear right foot (I am right-handed) along with an abbreviated backswing, this ended up becoming one of my favorite shots to make. If you put the ball too far back on your right foot the ball is invariably shanked, so ball position is critical as well.

I soon began to loosen up and improvise a bit. I don't like going over trees because I've always had a low trajectory. I am able to hit my 4-Hybrid by keeping it low and weaving my way between or under trees successfully. Once on the Par 4 15th hole of Bayonet, I found my tee shot in the trees on the left on hardpan. The green was even further left, making the approach difficult. By keeping my 4-hyrid low and intentionally hooking the ball, I was able to get through the trees and land smack dab on the extremely challenging green to two-putt for par. These creative shots give me the most fun and satisfaction.

Another situation that I was able to execute well was fairway bunker shots. These were far less intimidating to me than greenside bunkers. I exclusively use my 7-iron in these situations because it is the club I feel most comfortable with. I stay well-balanced with a quiet lower body and make clean contact with the ball. Greenside bunkers, however, became a source of neurosis. I would do anything to avoid them and my heart sank whenever I found myself in one. I automatically assumed an extra one or two shots would be added to my score – definitely not a good mental approach to have walking up to my ball.

The mental part about having to hit a sand shot was the bigger issue for me, but I also failed to follow some of the basic technique. I had the ball too far back in my stance. I had a hard time grasping setting up my body to the left of the target line – I didn't want it to go left because it would keep going left I believed. I would de-loft the club because opening the face just freaked me out – I assumed with such a wide open face I would shank it. I always failed to keep the club-head open and moving through the sand.

I bought five different sand wedges because each promised to help me get out of bunkers "like no other club." Well, none worked. What did work was learning proper technique. I don't believe that one piece of advice will change your entire game, but sometimes a little nugget can help one aspect of your game. I saw an interview about bunker play with Henrik Stenson, the Swedish golfer and 2013 Tour Champion and FedEx Cup Champion. Stenson said that when in the bunker in a practice session, hold the club-face open and take a scoop of sand. When you take the wedge back, the sand should still be on the club-face until it bypasses your shoulder. I tried this over and over again in a practice session. I finally grasped how open the club-face should remain throughout the shot. When I played the course, I was getting out of bunkers like never before and even better, I looked forward to the challenge of playing out of a sand trap. Now that I know what to do and have had good results to back it up, the intimidation factor has been eliminated.

As for chipping and pitching, I studied and practiced with determination but it seemed like every time I got into a particular situation, my mind went blank. For example, in fluffy rough, I would make a descending blow. From my instruction, I was supposed to stand taller and grip down on the club with a wider stance while hitting the ball – not the ground. I always hit the darn ground and the ball didn't travel very far. And forget about me recognizing a flyer lie. I was too busy being excited about finding my ball teed up to take into account what that meant. Only when I was right in the middle of my swing would I think "Uh oh, too much club!" and the ball would go flying over the green. Mastering the short game, pitching and chipping in particular, is the greatest challenge for most recreational golfers based on what I have seen playing several hundred rounds.

Despite so much play, little things continued to flummox me. When the ball was above my feet, I froze, not remembering what to do. I failed to stand taller at address and did not aim far enough to the right because I kept questing "Hmm, do I hit more to the right or more to the left?" My brain was a jumble of golf information and that can happen when you try to cram a lifetime of learning in a few short months. I also froze when the ball was below my feet. I failed to have correct posture to make solid contact and I always lost my balance. Both situations have taken time to overcome but remain a challenge.

The same struggles occurred with downhill and uphill lies. I kept setting my shoulders in the opposite direction of the slope and losing my balance. Once I grasped that I had to swing the club with the slope, not against it, it dramatically improved my game.

Chipping from heavy rough around the green was one of the shots that could send me into a tantrum. I always put the ball too far back in my stance and had too much body movement. It took a long time for me to open the face slightly and stand with my weight centered while keeping my arms relaxed and mainly use my wrists. Once I did this successfully, I began to enjoy the challenge of chipping onto the green and seeing how close I could get the ball to the hole.

The enjoyment of golf grows exponentially when you know what to do. Even if it doesn't work out, having the knowledge and making the commitment raises the probability of a successful execution of the shot.

When the ball was just in the rough, I found success using Sir Nick Faldo's recommendation of popping it out of the grass with the toe of an 8-iron. To help clear my mind I carry a little laminated cheat sheet to remind me of the fundamentals but also to remind me of what to do in particular situations.

One Faldo lesson I read about was to never swing with more than 80 percent effort. That idea I struggled with for a long time but I soon learned that bashing the ball was not necessarily going to make it go farther. It only increased my chances for making errors. Once I grasped that the point was to get a "lovely" rhythm instead, I could hit my shots with relaxed ease and still flight them as far as I wanted. Direction over distance began to make sense to me. Soon, distance followed because I was using the proper technique.

Faldo also said to aim my chin at the ball. This allowed me to keep my head down, which has been one of my biggest struggles. It's not that I am eager to see where my ball lands, I have a difficult time physically staying down over the shot.

When hitting the ball, Faldo recommended visualizing sandpaper. The first time I heard this, I dismissed it because frankly I couldn't figure out how to compress the club-face against the ball to make it go forward while creating the friction to make the ball spin. Faldo said that he had picked up the tip while watching Lee Trevino. He recommended keeping the club-head moving down through the target line, keeping your hands ahead of the club-head through impact. When practiced extensively this worked, however, I had from very early on picked most of my shots clean because I always felt guilty about taking a divot on any golf course. Joe took dollar-sized divots and had great back spin on the ball into the green. I was barely able to pick out some tufts of grass.

Faldo also recommended something that I preferred to do: practice on the course. He said that working on the range was too limiting and didn't really give you a good sense of your shots and the ball never behaves the same way it would on the course. Faldo was talking about doing this practice not while playing a round of golf, but upon seeing an open hole or two, to go out there and practice. He also suggested doing something that appealed to me – feeling okay about having a different follow-through on different shots rather than expecting to have the same swing technique through each and every shot. This opened up a more creative approach to the game that made me feel confident and not so concerned about how my swing looked.

I also learned not to dramatically change the position of the ball in my stance. Doing so affects the swing. I hit my drives and fairway shots with the ball exactly in the middle. I used to position my tee shot closer to inside my left heel with reduced success.

Only when you have played golf for a while do you get (hopefully) to the realization that golf is a journey not a destination. I thought once I started playing there would be a sense of "having arrived" but that never happened even after my birdies or hole-in-one. This is where golf is like life. You have high moments, you have low moments but you just keep on that journey.

Joe said if I really wanted to be good, I had to practice every day. Practice just seems like a chore to me. When I golfed, I wanted to have fun not feel like I was at work.

Pro golfer Jerry Pate felt that maintaining a spirit of fun when working at your job (whatever that job may be) was how to enjoy life overall since work makes up such a large percentage of how we spend our lives. Many could be envious that his job was golf, but he could also fall into the rut of struggling at it and not taking much enjoyment from it. Part of his work involved practice, which can get boring, routine and be looked at as a chore rather than a means to an end. Pate felt it was his dedication to practice that contributed to his most memorable wins.

In 1981 at a tournament in Memphis Tennessee, Pate told the press that if he won the event, he would jump into the lake that hugs the 18th green, clothes and all. He had not won in a few years so it was a bold declaration. When Sunday afternoon rolled around, Pate holed a short putt for birdie and won the tournament by two strokes over Tom Kite and Bruce Lietzke. Pate calmly handed his putter and sun visor to his caddie, faced the lake and plunged in with a racing dive. He had confirmed ahead of time that the lake was deep enough to dive into without chance of injury. When he emerged, he was laughing with relief. Finally, he had won again. His ears filled with the booming cheers of the gallery. It was not a major victory but it was a heady moment. The dry spell was over, quenched by the water at the 18th green.

Pate savored the moment. He felt a deep sense of appreciation and he was reminded how much fun it was to feel the thrill of winning. Knowing that he was the best golfer – even just for that week – was the greatest feeling. That is why he decided he would jump in the lake if it happened because enjoying golf, having fun with it and experiencing the joy of it was as important as making a living at it. He knew, however, that practice is what had got him there, just as practice had helped him win the 1976 US Open at the Atlanta Athletic Club, his rookie year on the PGA Tour.

Pate was paired with John Mahaffey, who was only one stroke behind him. If Mahaffey tied him by the final hole, there would be an 18-hole play-off the next day. The pressure was on Mahaffey to tie. After a decent drive, he didn't hit his second shot well. It skidded right into the lake. The pressure was then off Pate. All he needed was a par to win. His tee shot had landed in the rough and he had a flyer lie. The pin was about 190 yards away and was tucked into the left front part of the green near the lake. Pate's caddie suggested a four-iron. Pate insisted on the 5-iron instead, aware that his adrenaline was pumping hard. To avoid getting tangled in the rough, Pate took the club back a little more inside the line than he normally would. He hit the ball cleanly and it went straight for the pin. It landed two feet to the left of the cup. The gallery exploded and Mahaffey graciously congratulated him. Pate sunk the short birdie putt and won the US Open by two strokes.

Looking back on that day in 1976 at the Atlanta Athletic Club, Pate only regretted that he didn't have the awareness then to celebrate his major victory by diving into the lake. That is why he wasn't going to let the opportunity slip by in Memphis, even if it wasn't a major event. Enjoyment was an important part of the game, whether playing or practicing and you have to grab onto that enjoyment when it presents itself.

Golf – as in life – is all about attitude.

CHAPTER FIFTEEN

Confidence

A lot of people have good luck charms. We have all heard about athletes possessing something that makes them feel confident and helps them believe in what they are doing. Recreational golfers are no different. When I hit my hole-in-one shot I was wearing a Tiger Woods cap. I believed that was my good luck charm and I never play a round of golf without it.

Anyone who knows how difficult the game of golf is can appreciate what Woods has accomplished. He has an intimidating presence on the course, like a stalking panther, that adds to his mystique but in those early days he was just a lean kid with a lot of enthusiasm – along with a phenomenal game.

As a teenager, Woods wasn't a robot, thinking only about golf. He collected coins and enjoyed listening to music and said he loved fishing.

About a year after turning pro, Tiger Woods publicly said he hoped that kids would think that playing golf was cool. He had won more than a hundred trophies by the time he was 15 years old – of course that was cool! He said he wanted to be the best ever – the Michael Jordan of golf. For him that meant challenging Jack Nicklaus's major record. In 1990 when he played with touring pros at a pro-junior event, he shot a 69, beating 18 of the 21 professional golfers. Tiger Woods was on his way.

Unlike a lot of pros, I never got one shred of instruction out of watching Tiger's game that I could apply to my own game. For me, Tiger Woods is an example of confidence. Having confidence on the course is one of the most important aspects of the game and it was something I had struggled with my entire life. With practice and knowing what to do, confidence is easier to come by but still, you have to have the inner fortitude and belief in yourself. The dichotomy is that confidence stems from playing well.

Yet, no matter how good you are, in today's world the media and fans always seem to be looking for who will challenge the top player. Names are bandied about; rivalries are invented even when records simply don't match up.

Back in Ben Hogan's day, the media lauded the young upstart Gardner Dickinson as a threat to "the old man."

Gardner was a huge fan of Ben Hogan. He chain-smoked like Hogan. He emulated Hogan on the course by studying shots with the same great care and focus. He was downcast on bad shots like Hogan. He even dressed like Hogan. As an ardent disciple of the greatest golfer of that era, Gardner even once worked as Hogan's assistant. But what about his game?

At the 1955 Los Angeles Open (now the Northern Trust Open) Gardner Dickinson looked like he was on his way to winning, but he faltered on the final round and another youngster named Gene Littler went on to win. The media then pushed the story that Dickinson and Littler were challengers to the old guard, even billing them as a "safe bet."

Gene Littler strolled around so casually it hardly appeared he was even playing a round of tournament golf. He frequently yawned and sometimes appeared to be half asleep during the most intense moments of competition.

Born in San Diego, Littler broke par by age 14 and became a National Amateur Champion in 1953 before turning pro in the spring of 1954. He had a brilliant showing at the US Open when he came in second place.

The next year he won four times before struggling on and off for the next several years until he won five times on the PGA Tour in 1959 and then had a crowning achievement as winner of the 1961 US Open at Oakland Hills Country Club (South Course) in Bloomfield Hills, Michigan. He would rack up 50 professional wins and become a World Golf Hall of Fame member in 1990.

Though he had a good career, Littler was not the dominant player the media had predicted him to be, but American players were not the only focus in seeking out young stars. The media also looked to the southern hemisphere and took notice of young Peter Thomson. They called him the best foreign golfer to come along since South African Bobby Locke.

Built like a fullback, Thomson did not bomb it far. However, his play on British and Australian courses had honed his short game and that made him a lethal player. He won the Open Championship five times in the course of a dozen years. It was not as if the field wasn't deep during those years with Palmer, Hogan, Player, Locke and many others nipping at his heels.

His final Open win at Royal Birkdale Golf Club in 1965 was a victory over the elements as much as the field. The 36 year old Australian battled violent winds and multi-directional rain to win by two strokes over Welshman Brian Hugget and Ireland's Christy O'Connor.

Gary Player quit after firing a 79 in the morning round.

"My neck hurt too much," Player said. He had just come off the US Open win at Bellerive Country Club and his well-conditioned body had taken a beating.

Nicklaus, the Masters' champion that year (and strong pre-tournament favorite), started the final day with a bogey six and then his game went from bad to worse. Palmer had an even tougher time.

"I am sick," Palmer said. "My putting was atrocious."

Thomson, a mild-mannered, tight-lipped man with a reportedly deep-seated antipathy for the American tour, took the third round lead from Tony Lema and fellow countryman Bruce Devlin in the morning's impossible conditions. Then, in the afternoon final round with the rain subsiding but the wind still whipping hard, Thomson showed his mettle. He moved three shots in front with nine holes to play. Lema first and then Roberto De Vicenzo made alternate charges at him. Lema birdied the 13th to move within one stroke of the Australian and had a 12-foot putt on the 16th that would have tied him with his playing partner. The putt hit the cup but lipped out.

"That putt killed me," Lema said later.

De Vicenzo four-putted the ninth hole.

Thomson increased his advantage with a birdie on 17 and clinched with a par on the final hole where Lema bogeyed.

"I want the sixth jug," Thomson said without emotion. Only Harry Vardon had won it six times and Thomson was keen on matching the immortal Englishman.

"It was the greatest of my five Open wins," he continued, "because I was up against the toughest field this time, a field with great golfers."

Thomson would be denied a sixth win and not win another major. He was inducted into the World Golf Hall of Fame in 1988 having won 82 professional tournaments.

The fourth place finisher in that 1965 Open Championship was Roberto De Vicenzo.

"I am lazy – no punch at the end," De Vicenzo complained.

The long-hitting Argentine didn't have to wait too long for his major victory. Though Jack Nicklaus won the Open the next year at Muirfield, Roberto took the Claret Jug the following year at Royal Liverpool Golf Club. It's not as if Roberto had been lazy – not at all. He had been trying to win a major title for twenty years so when he beat the field that final day in July he was elated, having reached the climax of his career.

De Vicenzo won the 1967 Open dramatically, staving off tremendous pressure and hanging on to his lead. At one point he was four strokes ahead of Jack Nicklaus but the margin narrowed and the tension mounted. The high point came at the 16th hole. First Jack birdied the par five cutting the lead to two shots. Roberto, playing just behind Jack, drove way to the right where a vast expanse of out-of- bounds territory awaited a gambling or wayward shot. De Vicenzo chose to gamble. He took out a wood and lofted the ball over the trouble to the heart of the green. He two-putted for a matching birdie and all but clinched the title.

"Well, we thought it would happen sometime," he said. "I felt like an Englishman today. I wanted to win. I felt everybody wanted me to win although they had their own man in the field."

Though the Open was his only major, Roberto De Vicenzo won more than 230 titles worldwide and was inducted into the World Golf Hall of Fame in 1989.

Many thought De Vicenzo would be a bigger threat in the majors or even dominate the US Tour but it never materialized. Even pros can't pick out the next star or dominant player. For a time in the 1950s, pros had their eyes on young Bud Holscher. He was built like a basketball player, tall and lanky and could bomb a drive like no one else. He also had excellent putting and chipping skills, but Holscher would be limited to 3 professional wins because he got down on himself which led to his game spiraling out of control.

Around the time Holscher was trying to win, the media began to note that life for a touring pro was reaching a turning point.

In the early days of American golf, players rose up through the caddie ranks before becoming assistants in the pro shop. They had to battle to find money just to afford to play one tournament. Most pros slept in their cars to avoid having to pay for a hotel room. Ben Hogan said he lived on oranges for four days and the last amateur to win the US Open, Johnny Goodman, said he caught a cattle train just to make it to a tournament.

The mid 1950s was a time when golfers who were emerging out of college were being scouted as aggressively as promising football players. Signed by sporting goods companies, the players didn't have to be so desperate about making some money to fund their tournament travel, but those who found a sponsor were the most comfortable. It was a time when golf was starting to be a good way to make a living but it also brought about a new set of pressure. Just the thought of losing a tournament was stressful. Gardner Dickinson admitted to thinking about the $5,000 winning check when his lead slipped away at the Los Angeles Open. It was good money – but you had to win to get it.

Those who had no sponsors or endorsements still had to work hard to scrape enough money to get into tournaments. A war veteran named Palmer Lawrence dreamed of becoming a golf pro while in the foxholes of Korea. He saved money for four years just to make it to the tour, but he failed to do well, lost all his money and returned to a quiet civilian life.

Another ex-military man was also interested in a golf career. Orville Moody was a sergeant in the US Army for fourteen years. He decided to pursue a military career after failing to secure a sponsor to fund his dream of becoming a golf professional, but his service to America did not dampen his dream and he often played golf during those 14 years in the Army. Sometimes he would play 54 holes in one day. Sure enough, he began beating the best players in US Army golf events. When touring pros would visit the base for exhibition matches, Moody would step up wanting to take on the best in the game. Sometimes he even won. The pros he met encouraged him to pursue golf when he got out of the Army but by that time, Moody was in his mid thirties.

Moody began to feel dissatisfied about his life and at the prompting of his wife, quit the Army to pursue the pro circuit. Sponsors were lining up to back the ex Army man with the reputation of having beaten touring pros, but in his first few outings, Moody had poor showings and questioned whether leaving the Army had been a wise decision. One of the pros reminded him that "quitters never win" and Moody continued to pursue his dream. He chipped away at the obstacles that kept him from winning, like self-doubt and physical fatigue. By August of 1968 he won a tournament and it gave a big boost to his confidence.

Having virtually no major tournament experience, Moody then got into the 1969 US Open in Houston Texas through local and sectional qualifying, emboldened by his 1968 win and with a "nothing to lose" attitude. By the final round, he found himself three strokes off the lead. Moody put his foot on the gas and took over the lead with just six holes to play. But then his self-confidence faltered. The idea of winning the US Open was overwhelming. On the 13th hole, Moody had a four foot putt for birdie that would give him a two shot lead. He blew the putt. Then on the 14th he sent his tee shot into the rough, got a bogey and slipped back to find himself in a tie. He blew another birdie opportunity at the 16th hole and his confidence took a serious blow. He managed to make par at 17, but walked to the 18th tee discouraged. As he was teeing up his ball, word came that the co-leader, Miller Barber, had faltered. Moody was now in the lead. A par four on the final hole would win him the US Open. Confident, Moody bombed a 310 yard drive right down the fairway. He then hit his approach shot 12 feet from the pin. With his heart pounding, he stroked his putt. It stopped a foot from the hole. He could barely contain himself as he hovered above the putt and with all the focus and control he could muster, Moody sank the putt to win the 1969 US Open. The gallery went nuts. The former Army man, not young by any means, had captured the ultimate dream.

It was rumored that prior to the tournament, defending champion Lee Trevino had picked Moody to win, describing Moody as "one hell of a player."

Another professional whose golf dreams were intermingled with military service was Lou Graham. Graham served as a member of the Old Guard, Company E of the Third U.S. Infantry Regiment, the ceremonial Honor Guard that guards the Tomb of the Unknown Soldier in Arlington National Cemetery. After the Army, having won the Inter-Service Championship as a member of the golf team, Graham joined the PGA Tour in 1964. Three years later, he would score his first win, but the crowning achievement of his life was the 1975 US Open. He beat John Mahaffey in a play-off at Medinah Country Club in Medinah, Illinois.

John Mahaffey was no slouch. Three years later he won his first and only major, the 1978 PGA Championship where, after trailing Tom Watson by seven strokes with 14 holes to play, Mahaffey managed to get himself into a three-man play-off with Watson and Jerry Pate. All three players made par on the first playoff hole. The drama ended on the second playoff hole when Pate missed the green and Watson missed a 30-foot birdie attempt. Mahaffey sunk his 12-foot birdie putt to win the PGA Championship and his round is known as one of the best scrambles in PGA Championship history.

Major championship wins resonate throughout golf history and elevate a golfer to another stratosphere. Already a multiple major winner, Phil Mickelson's 2013 win at the Open Championship at Muirfield is an unforgettable example of tenacity and focus on a difficult course. At one of the Open press conferences, Mickelson alluded to the fact that he had "found something" but he was unwilling to share what that "special formula" for better play was. It wasn't the first time the golfing world had heard of a winning formula mentioned by a pro golfer.

For Cary Middlecoff, a trained dentist who happened to have one leg shorter than the other, the winning formula began to take shape in the second round of the 1955 Masters. He shot a 65 and upon returning to the locker room, he was grinning from ear to ear, feeling confident that he had figured out a secret to better putting. Unlike Phil Mickelson, Cary Middlecoff was willing to share.

"It's just a larger grip on the putter," he said.

Who could argue with Middlecoff? On the 13th green at Augusta he found himself 80 feet from the cup. He intensely studied the putt. He took his time, an act that would be repeated over and over again and give him a reputation as a slow player. With the gallery waiting with breathless if not impatient anticipation, he finally took his big fat grip in hand and stroked the ball. Where it would end up was anyone's guess as the green weaved this way and that, making the ball's final destination only a guess. The ball crested over a rise, took a turn and then put itself right into the hole as the crowd erupted. The cheers would continue all the way through the end of the round until Ben Hogan placed the green jacket on Middlecoff's shoulders.

Had Middlecoff found a winning formula? It's possible, at least for a time. Later that year he placed 2nd at the PGA Championship and the next year he won his second U.S. Open at Oak Hill Country Club (East Course).

The 2013 PGA Championship was also played at Oak Hill Country Club (East Course) in Rochester NY where Jason Dufner kept a steady calm exterior intact to take his first major. A sad display of poor etiquette outside the ropes by the gallery would no doubt have disconcerted the architect of Oak Hill, who was known as "the ogre who traps the pros."

Robert Trent Jones was labeled a "monster-creator" by professional golfers. His remodeling of Oak Hill (East Course) for the 1968 US Open was considered "ridiculously tough." Jones was unperturbed, declaring to writer Bill Bruns, "The golfer is the attacker and the architect is the defender. It is my job to see that the pros don't have it too easy."

Jones had been intent on making the game a more demanding one for the pros ever since he began designing courses in 1930. While weekend golfers might boast of breaking 100 on a Jones course, his strategically placed hazards spawned a continuing feud between him and many of the big-name pros.

"The pros are pampered," Jones shot back at the critics. "If they ran the tour, they would shoot 250 for 72 holes! They play all year long on easy courses and when they can't break par they look for the nearest villain – the architect."

Jones had endured some stiff criticism by the pros in 1951 when he was called in to set up the Oakland Hills course for the US Open in Bloomfield Hills, Michigan. Jones had lengthened most holes and re-trapped the fairways and greens to put a premium on accuracy. Some call Ben Hogan's 1951 US Open final day performance at Oakland Hills one of the greatest rounds ever played because of the difficult course set-up. Hogan may have faced over 160 of the world's best golfers that day, but the real battle was with Robert Trent Jones.

Oakland Hills was set up like it was full of land mines, except the mines were bunkers that gobbled up golf balls like a hungry monster. Hogan found the bunkers all day long and had to make precise approaches to avoid being severely penalized. It discouraged long straight drives, the very thing that Hogan excelled at. For players who had difficulty adapting and playing creative shots, they were all but dead from the first tee.

Hogan had prepared himself well having played five days of practice, but found himself frustrated on the first hole on the very first day of competition. He battled to figure out how to approach the green. He finally settled on a 2-iron, waggled only once and proceeded to soar the ball over the green. It wasn't a good start. The course made him feel stupid and he was steaming mad. He shot a disappointing 76 that first day.

With a steely mindset, Hogan went out the next two rounds and began adapting his game to the course instead of trying to fit the course to his game. He played well enough to find himself two strokes off the lead. Back then the US Open concluded on Saturday, so after his morning round, Hogan had to go back out in the afternoon.

After his lunch break, Hogan stepped out onto the first tee focused on the task at hand. He was pissed off at the course set-up, but he did not allow it to unnerve him. He was determined to beat "The Monster" but he wasn't aggressive. He slowly chipped away at the course and after the first nine holes was even par.

On the 10th hole Hogan had a decent drive but his approach could have been considered the shot of the tournament. The ball sailed 200 yards right at the pin, leaving him a short birdie putt. Now one under par for the round, Hogan was feeling emboldened, but he did not allow the thrill of the shot to knock him off track. He still had a long way to go and he was determined to stay focused.

On the short 13th hole, Hogan bagged another birdie that jolted the gallery to cheers but Hogan refused to celebrate. He was determined to remain focused. The packed gallery slumped their shoulders and moaned as he bogeyed 14, but were jubilant once more as he birdied 15. He made it to the 18th hole still two under par. Hogan's ball laughed as it flew 250 yards over the bunkers Jones had built to ensnare him. A deftly hit 6-iron cleared more bunkers and the shot came to rest about 14 feet from the pin. With the crowd breathless and fraught with desire to erupt, Hogan sunk his birdie for a three under 67 final round. It was an explosive win. Hogan's final score matched his US Open win the year before at Merion, 7 over.

As Hogan walked up to the clubhouse, he saw the wife of the architect, Robert Trent Jones. "Oh Ben," she cried, "what a marvelous round!"

Hogan turned, his eyes smoldering from beneath his familiar white cap and snapped, "If your husband had to play the courses he built, you would both be on the bread line!"

Hogan later said that if he had to play Oakland Hills every week he would have found another way to make a living.

Robert Trent Jones did not look like the ogre the pros painted him out to be, as if he was rubbing his hands together and snickering while fiendishly plotting a way to make pros look like fools. He was short and fat with a cherubic face and had a mellow voice. He considered himself to be "the protector of golf." He believed that softening the course softened the game and therefore, destroyed its character.

After hearing all the criticism Jones said, "The pro wants fairway traps from where he can reach the green. He wants dead flat greens with no rolls or contours. He doesn't want any hole too long or the rough too deep. He gets his way often and a lot of tournaments are just boring putting contests. The PGA has the idea that galleries are attracted by low scores. They are not. What people want to see is great golf shots under truly tough conditions. They want drama."

Jones deplored the fact that par was steadily losing its significance. "When the pros can't reach a Par 5 in two shots, they start griping," he said. "I don't like cheap birdies. But oh how the pros scream. If they scored a five from 480 yards, they would have a bogey instead of a par. It doesn't take guts for a pro or an amateur to win on a soft course. A winner is a good player knowing how to finesse the ball from position to position on a tough course."

That is precisely why Ben Hogan's win at Oakland Hills is considered such a great achievement.

CHAPTER SIXTEEN

Grinding

For a while, Ben Hogan dominated the US Open – having won it four times between 1948 and 1953. When the US Open was held once again at Baltusrol in 1954 after an 18 year hiatus, the press thought the course was right up Hogan's alley.

The course had a long and notable history in the US Open.

The US Open at Baltusrol Golf Club (original course) in Springfield New Jersey in 1903 was the first of three consecutive wins by Willie Anderson of Scotland (he'd win a total of four as he had already taken the major in 1901 at Myopia Hunt Club in South Hamilton, Massachusetts). Ninety-three players started in the annual contest, the entries being the same as 1902. Twenty amateurs had entered. The course was playing a length of 6,003 yards and the continuous rain over the previous three weeks had rendered the greens soggy. The competition, however, was played in fine weather and the course continued to dry as the event progressed.

In the first round, the lowest score was 73 made by Willie Anderson. Defending Champion Laurence (Laurie) Auchterlonie came in with a 74. It appeared that at the 9th hole, after he pitched his ball onto the green, the ball embedded. Laurie loosened his ball (being under the impression that the rules allowed him to do so) but he was wrong and was penalized by one stroke. Under the old Rule 13 he may have been allowed to replace his ball.

Anderson continued in the second round with a 76 and by the completion of the third round had a six stroke lead, leading everyone to the conclusion that Anderson had wrapped up the US Open. However fellow Scot David Brown was also playing well.

Anderson was sailing along until he got to the short ninth hole (182 yards) after hitting his tee shot into the trees on his left. He appeared to display very bad judgment by trying to play through the narrow opening in the trees. The ball hit the branches and bounded back onto the stones. He failed to dislodge his ball on the next shot and then got out around the green on his fifth, pitched up onto the putting green on his sixth and ran down two putts, making eight for the hole.

The pressure was now intense because if Anderson bogeyed any more holes his chance of winning the US Open was gone. But Anderson was steely. At the seventeenth he needed a four or he would have had to make a three on the difficult home hole. After his drive, he hit his iron shots well twice and then needed a long putt. He sank the putt to tremendous cheers. He parred the 18th hole and tied David Brown's score, forcing a play-off.

Eighteen holes were played on Monday (Sunday was reserved for member play) and Anderson shot an 82 to Brown's 84. The conditions that day were entirely against good golf. Rain fell continuously and the fairways were filled with pools of water. The greens were soggy and soft. The advantage went to Anderson because it suited his style of play better than it did Brown's. Anderson pitched up boldly while Brown hit low approaches looking for roll.

Brown was crushed by the loss. A roofer by trade, he had pursued a career in professional golf from Scotland to England to Boston after his Open Championship win in 1886 when John Anderson, who was secretary of the Musselburgh Club at the time, invited him to play and even provided him with clothing to play in the event. Brown shocked the professionals by winning.

David Brown lost most of his wealth during the Wall Street Crash of 1929 and returned to Musselburgh Scotland, where he died the following year.

When the 1936 US Open was played at Baltusrol Golf Club (upper course), several players, including Johnny Revolta, grinded their way around the course in a practice round. Walter Hagen had yet to show up but when he did it was evening so he only played a few holes in the fading light.

A superb putter in his prime, Hagen had the ability to run up long approach putts in such a casual fashion you took it for granted that he would sink every putt. When he did fail to drain his putts, his face did not change. He would simply erase the missed putt from his mind and turn his thought to what he could do on the next hole.

Hagen, a raconteur with an indomitable spirit for life, was in a nostalgic mood at the event, recalling for the press stories from the last time the event had been held at Baltusrol 21 years earlier when amateur Jerome Travers won. Now, upon his return to Baltustrol in the first round, he reached 15 greens in regulation.

"That's better than I did last time," Hagen smiled. "But I believe I played with a little more confidence back then. There weren't so many possible winners in the field. I'd like to have the confidence to feel that this was 'my show' as I did then. But I like to see those youngsters up there. Maybe I was just a fresh kid to the old-timers years ago, but the youngsters of today are making the game bigger and bigger. More power to them but just as a reminder, don't count the 'old Haig' out for keeps."

But Hagen's major wins were long behind him. The field was filled with fresh talent. One player in particular stood out on that final day.

Tony Manero, a pint size New Yorker of Italian descent, came blazing down the fairways with a record smashing final round of 67 and an unprecedented at the time 282 to win the US Open.

Under a blistering sun, Manero accomplished at the time what was considered the greatest finish under fire in golf history.

Manero's finish over Harry Cooper was a dramatic comeback of almost hopeless odds. Until the 11th hour, the title was all but conceded to Cooper. Manero had been four strokes behind Cooper. Some members of the gallery had already left, telling people that Cooper had won the US Open.

Gene Sarazen did play a big part in Manero's heroic finish. Until the end of the third round, there was only one person at the event who thought Manero had a chance to win and that was Manero. He even bet $100 across the board on himself. At lunch time, after the morning round, Sarazen joined Manero's previous one-man band. He had been paired with Tony on that final day and watching Manero play, Sarazen said, "I'm playing with the next champion."

When they started the fourth and final round that afternoon, Sarazen said to Manero, "Come on, let's get that title." Gene blazed away with a 33, three under par, and Tony matched him shot for shot. Sarazen faltered on the home stretch, but the magic was still with Manero.

The tragic figure of the tournament was Harry Cooper who broke the former US Open record by two strokes but then had to sit in the clubhouse and hear the crowd cheer another champion. Cooper had played the first three rounds 71-70-70 but cracked under pressure coming home and finished with a 73 – not earth shattering but not good enough to hold up against Manero's game. He was crushed.

"I guess it's just not in the cards for me to win," he said, still haunted by his last US Open play-off loss in 1927.

Though sympathetic toward Cooper, it was hard to not feel happy for Manero. Just six years before he had been ill and dead broke. When he landed a job with the Sedgefield Country Club in Greensboro NC, it was his first regular professional job. Now he was a US Open Champion.

Sportswriter Jack Bell lamented the slipping of the old guard. He had the audacity to ask tour player Al Espinosa why veterans can't putt as well as they did a few years ago (this after Al had three-putted himself out of the tournament).

"I don't know," Al said, sadly. "The hole looks just as big. You line up the putts just the same, stroke just the same and you're sure they are all right. But they don't go in."

Al's wife had slipped and fallen in a theater a few days before and was limping around the course trying to follow her husband for moral support. Her hip finally got to rest when Al missed the cut.

Lots of quirky things were going on during the event. On Friday during the second round, Scottish golfer Bobby Cruickshank got into trouble right away. He bogeyed the second hole, double-bogeyed the third hole and on the fifth he got into an argument with his caddie and hit one over the green, ending up five over par for five holes. His wife glumly remarked from the gallery that her husband was about to throw a fit any minute.

Pro Leslie Madison, who was paired with Cooper, lost his wallet and watch to a pick-pocket as the crowds surged around the players.

When Sarazen and Manero came off the 18th tee after the third round, the fans were still following Sarazen into the lunch room. The facility hadn't been set up too well to accommodate and control the 10,000 fans in the gallery.

The weather had at least held up but became too hot and everyone was seeking shade. The course, however, was brutal. Eddie Williams, a well-known Miami pro who failed to qualify for the final round lamented, "The difference between me and Paul Runyan (two-time PGA Champion) is that on the 10th and 11th holes he needed five shots and I needed 10."

Some pros literally have nightmares after playing in a US Open. That was the case of Terchi Toda, the Japanese pro who had managed to find almost every single sand trap at the US Open at Oakmont back in 1927 and he failed to make the cut at Baltusrol in 1936.

"I see sand traps in my sleep and the next day my ball sees sand traps all day long," Terchi said.

The course set-up had caused fits so when the US Open returned to Baltusrol (lower course) in 1954 it carried with it a lot of anxious history. It had been lengthened to 7,027 yards and a par 70 (the members play the lower course at 6,501 yards). Ben Hogan, however, was not intimidated.

"There's no question in my mind that there might be a new record," he said. "The greens are wonderful and you can hold them with almost any shot. The fairways, traps and rough are perfectly fair for a test of golf."

Hogan was high on confidence. He had won three majors in 1953 and the only reason he didn't have a chance to win the 1953 PGA Championship was because it overlapped with the Open Championship that year. Otherwise, Hogan may have won all four majors that miracle year.

Sam Snead, hoping to capture the only major that had eluded him, was hampered by a sore neck and shoulder muscles. He felt miserable during the practice round on Monday and apparently became so cranky that his caddie laid down Snead's clubs at the fourth hole and quit. A replacement caddie was rushed out to ensure that Snead could finish.

By the final round, Ben Hogan was two strokes off the pace and the crowd was largely behind him to capture his fifth US Open in just seven years. But by lunch, blood had been shed.

Sportswriter Red Smith wrote that Hogan was in great trouble "worse than the worst Rocky Marciano suffered at any time." Both champion athletes happened to be competing in defense of their title that same Thursday when the golf tournament began – the golfer who was once a fist-fighter and the fist-fighter who had taken up golf for fun. Rocky got his ordeal over in an hour but Hogan had an adversary "that wouldn't fight back, a mute and stubborn little white ball that just sat there staring back at him." Smith could also have been referring to one of Hogan's playing competitors.

Probably the most non-talkative golfer to walk a fairway was a lean 37 year old teaching professional from Clayton Missouri named Ed Furgol. Not once during the three days had Furgol engaged in conversation of more than two or three words between shots. He was a tight-lipped man with a purpose.

When he walked, Furgol's left arm was bent stiffly at the elbow, palm turned back and slightly outward. He had shattered his elbow as a child and the arm was left permanently crooked, almost withered. The doctor who treated him suggested he try golf. His locked in position left arm helped him hit the ball true to the target. Over a thousand rounds as a teaching professional, Furgol had averaged a 71.5 score but had never won a big championship. Now was his chance. Furgol had been focused on making pars at Baltusrol and it was paying off on that last day. He had taken the lead and Hogan had fallen back. On the 18th he hooked his drive into the trees, but his crooked arm helped guide his 7 iron and get out of trouble. Gene Littler was one stroke behind him but failed to hole an 8 foot putt on the 18th to tie. The title belonged to Ed Furgol. Finally, he opened his mouth to speak.

"My left elbow was a little stronger than Hogan's," he joked. "It kept me out of the rough." Then he got serious, addressing his stone-face personality. "Golf is my work and I didn't want anything to distract me from a shot that might make a difference. That is why I never talked to anybody, not even my caddie."

To be able to beat Hogan and a strong field was significant to Furgol and the highlight of his career (he also played on the 1957 Ryder Cup team). It was his only major win and one of six professional wins. Ben Hogan would never again win a major.

*

The site of Ben Hogan's impossible 1951 win at Oakland Hills Country Club (South Course), also served as the site of the 1996 US Open. Then, Steve Jones' win was called "unexpected" and "unlikely" and was the highlight of his 11 professional wins thus far.

Jones had not played in the US Open since missing the cut in 1991 and his career had mostly been hampered by injury. He did not play in any majors until he showed up at the 1996 US Open after advancing through sectional qualifying.

When the tournament began, Jones felt at peace, but also inspired. A friend had given him Curt Sampson's book *Hogan*. One of the things he got from the book was that Hogan was always trying to get a birdie and he would not back down no matter what. He would just focus on each and every shot. Jones felt that he had absorbed the lessons of Hogan's life and game and now here he was playing at the very course Hogan had his astonishing win. This elevated Jones to a steady start and an extraordinary finish. He birdied the 9th and 10th holes that got him into a tie with a man he greatly admired, Tom Lehman. By the 12th hole, he had a two shot lead when Lehman bogeyed and he made birdie out of a greenside bunker.

The real test came down to the 18th hole. Both players were tied again. Lehman pulled a driver and his caddie balked, suggesting a 3-wood. But Lehman went ahead and hit driver anyway. The ball ended up in a bunker right near the front lip. Despite Lehman's shot, Jones also chose to hit driver and hit it smartly over some bunkers and in the fairway down the right side. Lehman was forced to lay up while Jones hit a wicked 7-iron onto the green. When he got up there, he asked his brother Scott, who was on the bag, how he stood. Jones had to two-putt from 14 feet for the victory. He missed his first putt by 18 inches but sunk that for the victory.

Tom Lehman was gracious, despite having suffered yet another heartbreak in recent tournament play. "I'm not sure you realize what it would be like to miss three years of golf right in the middle of your career," he said of Jones. "For Steve to come back and win the U.S. Open, to me, is just an incredible story."

Who knows if Ben Hogan was watching the telecast of that US Open in 1996 (he died a year later), but Steve Jones certainly believed either through his own pure imagination or divine intervention that Ben Hogan had propelled him to that win.

Tied for 82nd was a young amateur named Tiger Woods.

*

The different locations on which the US Open is held contributes to the difficulty of the event. Cherry Hills Country Club in Cherry Hills Village, Colorado was the site of the 1938, 1960 and 1978 US Open. During the 1960 US Open, the higher elevation coupled with heat had pro golfers feeling the pressure. Balls travelled at least 10% farther and made club selection a guessing game, but the real test was stamina. At the "Mile High Open" many players had to sit or lie down in between shots. This made for slow play with sometimes up to 35 minute delays. They made oxygen tanks available, but it did little to appease the players. 1958 US Open Champion and 2002 World Golf Hall of Famer Tommy Bolt, known for his fiery disposition, was outraged at the conditions. On the first day, he hit two balls into a lake and then threw his driver in after them. "My head and hands are swollen!" he yelled. Bolt quit the tournament.

Other players worked hard to get acclimated to the course and the rarefied air. Suffering along with everyone else in the grueling conditions was Arnold Palmer.

"It took longer to get a full breath up there at first and I found myself using the wrong clubs," Palmer said. But once he got acclimated, he turned on his own heat. Palmer got six birdies on the first nine holes on his road to winning the 1960 US Open. A young amateur named Jack Nicklaus came in second place.

Tough conditions, tough circumstances or health challenges every golfer must face, even the recreational golfer and I was no different. A wisdom tooth began erupting in my jaw and after a tenacious infection and difficult surgery that left a quarter of the wisdom tooth still wedged in my jaw, I was laid-up for two months, unable to golf. Frustrated at not being able to play, all sorts of thoughts gathered in my head. Would I remember how to hit the ball? Had the progress I made in dropping my handicap evaporated?

I tried to distract myself – as I normally did when faced with life challenges – by reading about some of the oddities in the golf world. Some of the strangest stories revolve around the game of golf. Some are even tragic. We forget that sometimes clubs can literally be weapons – against ourselves.

In 1994, a 16 year old boy was killed when he bashed a bench with a golf club, the shaft broke, bounced back at him and went straight through his chest. In 2005, a 15 year old boy took a swing at a fire hydrant after finding a 5-iron. Part of the shattered club lodged in his neck. That same year, a 12 year old fell onto a broken club and died.

It is rumored that pro golfer Lefty Stackhouse once got so angry after a poor shot he punched himself in the chin, knocking himself out.

Another golfer was practicing his shots when a cloud of smoke rose up from the grass and he felt a sharp pain in his leg. His club-head had hit a .22 caliber bullet hidden in the grass, detonating it into his leg.

But it wasn't all injury or harm in the annals of oddities in the golf world. In 1981, Norman Manley, a maintenance worker, was noted for having racked up 46 hole-in-one shots, more than any pro or amateur golfer in the world. Once, he even shot back to back aces on par 4 holes. Manley insisted he never aimed for the pin, only attempted to get on the green. There were doubters about that remark. Pro golfer Art Wall was listed as having 42 aces and Wall said he always went for the pin. Others flat-out did not believe the number of Manley's aces, but he always had a witness to attest to the miracle shot. As of the current date, Manley still holds the record at 59 aces.

Oddities in golf are becoming more common as increased viewership and high-definition TV pick up a golfer's every move. When pro Brad Faxon teed off at the Honda Classic one year, a seagull grabbed his ball from the first fairway, flew off with it, only to drop it 40 yards away, inches from a water hazard. Fortunately tournament officials allowed Faxon to return his ball to where the gull had pilfered it. Tiger Woods faced much harsher scrutiny over an "oscillating" ball in 2013.

Nowadays, golfers are viewed as athletes. Given the rigors of golf it is surprising they were ever considered anything else. In an attempt to find out who are the smartest athletes, a researcher conducted a four-year study in which athletes took a series of standard IQ tests. The results were that the highest IQ scores went to bowlers and the lowest IQ scores went to golfers. The researcher theorized that many golfers were one-dimensional. They were not avid readers of books or newspapers and most were oblivious to current events. For every intelligent golfer, the researcher concluded (as there certainly were intelligent golfers) there were seven or eight who "just weren't very bright."

*

I used the time that I was laid up to study changing my equipment. I read all about the latest technology and how it could improve my game. Because changing my equipment will revolutionize my game, right? I had changed my ball to the Precept IQ and found more length off the tee. Joe countered that my improved game was the reason for my improved drives – it wasn't just the ball.

Of course balls aren't the only pieces of golf equipment that have gone through re-design over the last several decades. Years ago, a company developed metal for the face of a driver using material that was used by the military to penetrate enemy armor. The feedback from those who had used it was sensational. A PGA professional played a round with the driver and was bombing it further than he ever had before. A golfer in California won his first long-ball competition using the driver. A recreational golfer shot his first subpar round in two decades. On a practice range, one amateur hit a 420 yard tee shot (but it was believed he was a long hitter and got an assist from the wind). Another golfer claimed to have split his golf ball in half (a downside to those with a high club-head speed).

The phenomenal driver was not limited to its length but accuracy as well. The company claimed that a well-known pro was shaping shots around trees. Other pros who saw him wanted to abandon their current drivers but could not because of endorsement deals. The PR on the driver was that the accuracy came from the largest most forgiving sweet spot that had ever been invented. Any good golfer would be able to accurately draw or fade shots like a pro.

You could get the driver for under $200 and they recommended if you had a swing speed over 120 MPH, it was best to carry some extra balls. Of course, I wanted to immediately order the driver (now several years old), but decided against it since I already had three (*this is the one that is going to change my game!*) extra drivers sitting in the garage.

I was frustrated during my illness. I just wanted to get back out there and play a round. When that time came, we went to Blackhorse, Seaside, California. I hit a few balls on the range, but not enough to give me any confidence. I decided to just surrender to the process, let go and have fun. How could I expect much after being in bed for two months?

My legs were shaking. I was so nervous at being back on the tee box but I soon settled down and proceeded to shoot my lowest front nine ever. I became so excited, I faltered on the back 9 but overall, it was my best round to date.

There is an old saying "beware of the sick golfer" because something seems to take over a player's game when ill. Perhaps we are too fatigued to get in our own way.

Gene Sarazen once faced a ferocious bout of the flu. His tonsils had also been removed and he was feeling lousy. Unable to practice, he doubted he would be able to play at all when he was scheduled to play a match against Olin Dutra at a course in Florida. However, as soon as Gene teed off, he was burning up the course. How someone who feels lousy and hasn't had a day of recent practice can dust the field remains one of the great mysteries in golf. In most other sports, Sarazen would have been beaten but for some reason, good golf can emerge when you need it most.

Bobby Jones believed that practice was how you got there. A poor player cannot play well when they are sick. But a player who has practiced hard and is sick has a chance of playing well.

In tournament play, physical health is important but the amount of mental focus required is a challenge for anyone to maintain week after week. By the end of the season, it becomes difficult to concentrate on anything. Recreational golfers may not face the pressure of professional tournament play, but they do get caught up in trying so hard that they end up failing.

The counter argument is *Well, I practice hard, so why isn't my game great?* Because golf remains a game of imperfect for everyone.

The mental grind of the game is something all players have to manage. Tiger Woods has culled down his schedule to where he can attack a course with a fresh mind and body. Other players like 2013 Masters Champion Adam Scott have done the same. But it's not as if these players are lazing around – they are still practicing.

Bobby Jones wrote that golf does not require a great deal of physical energy – not even tournament golf – but it does require intense focus and concentration over a long period of time. Any career that requires that amount of mental focus wears on the body. For example, a surgeon may be standing in one place while operating and even have a team for support, but no one can give the surgeon the ability to concentrate on what they are doing. The hard objective in golf is to have that intense focus over every single shot.

The recreational golfer is not required to play for a living. We can play when we feel like it and we usually bring a certain amount of excitement with us to the golf course. But we often rob ourselves of that excitement with unrealistic expectations.

It seems to fly in the face of conventional wisdom, but what I learned more than anything during that illness is that time away from the game actually seems to make for a better golfer.

CHAPTER SEVENTEEN

The Masters

To me, the four majors in golf are national holidays. Each one has its own unique appeal. For many, including myself, The Masters reigns supreme. It is a week I take off, no matter what I am doing or what is going on in my life so I can focus on all the pre and post tournament events. To not have to look at sponsor logos or watch too many commercials or have to listen to clowns yelling from the gallery adds to the uniqueness of the event. The prestige, the pressure and the accomplishment of slipping on a green jacket is like no other tournament.

The first man to win a green jacket was Horton Smith. He is attributed with being the first professional golfer to study putting as a means to beat his opponents. Though a popular man to many, he was not without controversy. He served as president of the Professional Golfers Association of America from 1952 to 1954. During that tenure, boxing great Joe Louis arrived in San Diego to play on a sponsor's exemption in that city's golf tournament, but learned that he was banned under the PGA's "whites only" rule.

The action to implement the ban was undertaken by Horton Smith, who called the committee in San Diego to question why they had even invited Louis. Smith said that Louis could not play because the tournament was under PGA jurisdiction and only whites were allowed to play. Louis, understandably, was outraged and publicly compared Smith's belief in the white race to Hitler's belief in a super race. Smith said he would further investigate the dispute, but denounced Louis for making it a personal matter when Smith was "simply" enforcing the policy at the time. Fellow black golfer at the event, Bill Spiller, was also denied the right to play.

Spiller wasn't ignorant to whites-only rules. He was born in Tishomingo, Oklahoma and moved to Tulsa as a nine-year-old to live with his father. He was an excellent athlete, a two-sport star in high school but he was also a hot-head, particularly about racial inequality he witnessed in Oklahoma. He went on to Wiley College in Marshall, Texas where he earned an education degree. Spiller then moved to Southern California to earn a living as a teacher, but there wasn't enough pay so he worked as a railroad porter instead. A fellow porter challenged him to a game of golf and he soon became hooked. He started competing and winning blacks-only amateur golf tournaments. After being denied entry into the 1948 Richmond Open in Richmond, California by the PGA of America, Spiller decided to sue. Fellow black golfer Ted Rhodes joined him in the suit.

The basis of the lawsuit was that the golfers were denied the right to earn a living in the sport because the PGA was closed to non-white participants. Under the Taft-Hartley Act such rules were against the law. Shortly before the court date, the golfers withdrew their lawsuit in exchange for a promise from the PGA lawyer that the PGA would end discrimination. The PGA reneged on its end of the bargain and began sponsoring "invitational" tournaments. People of color were never invited.

When officials at the San Diego Open invited Joe Louis and Bill Spiller to play, they were unaware of the PGA's "Caucasians only" clause and were unaware that Spiller had previously sued the PGA for discrimination. Fortunately, Joe Louis would not keep quiet about it after Horton Smith excluded both men from the event. Louis took his story to popular newspaper columnist Walter Winchell. The story quickly gained national attention. Once again, Spiller threatened to sue. Once again, Horton Smith promised to change the rules. This time the PGA of America announced non-whites could play, but only if they were invited. Some sponsors began inviting black golfers, but the PGA segregation clause remained intact.

In 1960, Spiller's cause came to the attention of California attorney general (and future California Supreme Court Justice) Stanley Mosk. AG Mosk told the PGA of America that it would not be allowed to use public courses because of their policy. At the time, most tournaments were held on public courses which of course are funded by public funds. The PGA of America responded that was fine because going forward, they were going to restrict their events to private courses. Mosk began contacting state attorney generals around the country to inform them of the PGA's position. Finally, in November of 1961, thirty-five years before one of the most successful golfers of all time, Tiger Woods turned pro, the PGA of America relented and removed their segregation clause from their policy. It was too late for Spiller to pursue a professional career. He was then forty-eight years old.

In 2009, the PGA of America granted posthumous membership to Spiller, Rhodes, and John Shippen. The PGA also granted posthumous honorary membership to Joe Louis.

In September of 2013, Horton Smith's Masters' jacket sold for $689,229. It wasn't the first time a green jacket had been sold. Doug Ford's 1957 jacket sold for $62,967.

It was believed that Smith's jacket went for such a high bid because Smith was the winner of the inaugural Masters tournament and was also known as one of the "original ten" in the golfing world. Someone who understood the significance of that bought the jacket. They also understood the significance of golf history and maintaining the dignity and honor it is to receive a green jacket.

The 1943, 1944 and 1945 Masters were cancelled due to World War II. When the tournament was won in 1946 by Herman Keiser, many people asked, "Who is Herman Keiser?"

An unassuming, low-ranked player with no flair, Keiser had defeated the greatest players of the game like Hogan, Snead and Nelson to win the green jacket by one stroke, his only major amongst eight professional wins. So a Masters win does not belong exclusively to the well-known "big names."

A friendly puff of wind was credited with helping Jack Burke Jr. win the 1956 golf championship.

The 5'7" Burke from Texas surged from eight strokes behind to capture the green jacket at formidable Augusta National. With its 6,965 yards of wooded fairways and gigantic greens, Burke was able to wrestle his way to the top. A well-liked golfer by many, Burke's win was very popular, but that did not take away from the empathy felt for Ken Venturi, the 24-year-old auto salesman who had captured the golfing world's fancy playing as an amateur in the prestigious event.

The tournament was won – and lost – on the 71st hole. After 16 holes of the final round, Venturi and Middlecoff (playing separately) were tied at one over par. Burke was one stroke back. Middlecoff was short on 17 and chipped up. A puff of wind blew his first putt off line and he took two more to get down. That gave him double-bogey six and put him three over. A few minutes later Burke got on in two, 15 feet from the cup. He sunk his putt for birdie. In the next twosome was Venturi. His second shot rolled to the back of the green, paused at the top then trickled over. A chip and two putts for bogey resulted and suddenly the amateur from San Francisco who had led at the end of every round needed a birdie on the last hole to tie Burke. Venturi didn't get it.

Burke, who Middlecoff jokingly called "rookie of the year for seven years" had finally captured his first major after turning pro 16 years earlier.

Today, at the age of 90, Burke shares his permanent locker at Augusta National Golf Club with Tiger Woods.

Venturi had his heart broken again in 1958 and in 1960 when he was edged out both times by Arnold Palmer.

Venturi achieved success on tour and in broadcasting but never won the coveted green jacket. He was inducted into the World Golf Hall of Fame in 2013.

Art Wall Jr. won the 1959 Masters with a baseball grip and a glass-shafted mallet putter.

A quiet, modest man from Pennsylvania, Wall explained his grip. "When I first started playing, I never knew there was another way to hold the club."

He had emulated Mickey Mantle's style and it was working, so why change? The putter, however, was new. He replaced an old wooden-shafted blade he had carried for 10 years and had won eight PGA Tour events with up until that time.

The putter – with three dots on its head to warn against three putts – played a major part on that final day.

Starting six strokes back and in a tie for 13th place, Wall birdied five of his six last holes for a total 284 that sent the pace-setters scrambling. Wall had leaped over 12 players in a spectacular surge.

The Masters had not seen a rally like that since Jack Burke in 1956 and again in 1957 when Doug Ford won with a final round 66, pushing ahead of three rivals.

Wall credited his caddie, Henry Hammond. "He helped make me a winner," Wall said. "To my mind, the 14th and 15th were the key holes and he set me straight on the 15th. I thought at first I'd use a four-wood for my second shot but he suggested a two-iron instead. I followed his advice and chose the iron. My shot landed about 25 feet from the hole. Frankly, I wasn't aware that I had five birdies in the last six holes until they told me about it later. I didn't even realize I had a chance to win until my playing partner Julius Boros told me I could take it all as we approached the 17th tee. When I heard a loud roar on the 15th hole, I figured Cary Middlecoff must have come up with an eagle three. Then when we came up to the 18th, all I was trying to do was get a par. I hit my best drive of the day, took a nine-iron and hit it about 12 feet from the flag. I looked that putt over a long time. It seemed to me it could go either way. So I played it straightaway and darned if the ball didn't go in!"

It was the only major of Wall's career in which he won 14 PGA Tour events.

In 1967, the Miami News heralded the fact that finally someone other than the big names had won The Masters (Palmer and Nicklaus dominated from 1960 to 1966 with one win going to Gary Player in 1961).

Some felt Gay Brewer deserved the win. It was just a year earlier that he had stood on the last green in the evening sunshine with two putts to win The Masters from 50 feet but flubbed his second putt from four feet. Brewer (alongside Tommy Jacobs) then lost in an 18 hole Monday play-off to the indomitable Jack Nicklaus.

Brewer wiped out that horrible loss in a sweeping charge over the lush green acres of Augusta National coming from two strokes back and jumping over three other players.

"I may be the happiest man in the history to win the Masters," the 35 year old graying Brewer said. "The Masters is really something special for me, especially after last year. I really wanted to win this one. I wanted to prove to myself that I had it in me to do it."

Brewer's triumph was a reward of long years of striving on the PGA Tour. When Jack Nicklaus placed the green jacket on Brewer in Bobby Jones Cabin, little did anyone know that the Nicklaus/Palmer domination era of The Masters had come to an end.

The next year, 1968, The Masters was fraught with controversy.

Bob Goalby had spent 11 years chasing his dream and found it that Sunday in an unexpected fashion. The 36 year old American and the 44 year old Robert De Vicenzo of Argentina finished the 72 holes in an apparent tie at 277. As plans were being made for a Monday play-off, tournament officials dropped a bombshell.

The Masters Rules Committee ruled that De Vicenzo had signed a wrong scorecard. De Vicenzo's playing partner Tommy Aaron marked a par-4 on the 17th hole when in fact De Vicenzo had made a birdie-3. De Vicenzo failed to catch Aaron's mistake and therefore signed an incorrect scorecard.

"Of course I am happy I won. I'd be a liar if I told you different,' Goalby said. "But I'm sorry I won it the way I did. I would have rather won it in a play-off."

Most Masters winners immediately start thinking about the US Open and the Open Championship but not Goalby. He wasn't even going to play in the Open Championship.

"It's not that I have anything against the British Open. It's a fine tournament. But I've always played here in the United States. I like the PGA-sponsored tournaments and I'm going to play in this country instead." Besides, he said, "I'm not too crazy about flying."

The man who incorrectly marked the scorecard to deny De Vicenzo the chance to win the 1968 Masters, Tommy Aaron, took the green jacket in 1973.

A mild-mannered soft-spoken man, a native of Georgia, Aaron felt great relief when he finally captured a major title 13 years after turning pro. He'd come up short plenty of times.

"It's no crime to finish second," he said. "After all, the greatest golfer in the world, Jack Nicklaus, has finished second 33 times (by 1973)."

Aaron had been runner-up 14 times prior to his 1970 win in the Atlantic Classic. It did little to change his image. Aaron was known on tour as a perennial bridesmaid, a choker, unable to close the big ones, but nothing compared to the criticism he received at the 1968 Masters for failing to record a proper score. One critic wrote, "Tommy Aaron, in his career, has devised innumerable methods to lose a tournament for himself. Today, he found a way to lose one for somebody else."

Very few people were interested in seeing Aaron ever wear the green jacket, particularly since he had not stood his ground and explained or apologized for the error he made. Aaron simply fled Augusta and refused to discuss it.

He was, however, almost a victim of an error that April in 1973. Examining his scorecard, he noticed that his playing partner, Johnny Miller, had given him a par five on the 13th hole when he actually had a birdie four. Aaron corrected it and saved a stroke penalty that could have cost him the tournament. Had Miller just made a mistake or was it intentional?

Washed out by rain on Saturday, the tournament had a dramatic climax with a spectacular late surge by Jack Nicklaus and a three-way battle down the stretch involving Aaron, JC Snead (nephew of Sam Snead) and Peter Oosterhuis (current TV commentator).

Having started the final day eight shots back of the leading Oosterhuis and with 13 other players in front of him, the Golden Bear knocked in birdies on four of the first six holes, added another at the long 8th and turned in 32 as thousands of fans swarmed to see what Jack would do on the back nine. But the charge by Jack simply was not enough. Nicklaus finished tied for third with Oosterhuis and Jim Jamieson. Aaron won one stroke over JC Snead (who the press referred to as a "strapping hillbilly").

Tommy Aaron had a career total of eight professional wins and was inducted into the Georgia Sports Hall of Fame in 1980 and the Georgia Golf Hall of Fame in 1989 but remained an unpopular figure in the world of professional golf.

By 1972, the only African-Americans visible at The Masters were those working as caddies and that brought out the critics. The tournament director, C.L. Davis, was miffed at the criticism, insisting he could not care less about race – only that the tournament attracted good golfers.

"We wish a black player would qualify," he said.

The tournament had undergone several rules changes, one of which was that any player who won a PGA sponsored match was eligible to participate in the Masters. At that time, there was also the rigorous "apprenticeship program" which usually took four years for a player to complete. Chuck Thorpe of Detroit Michigan was the only black golfer who had completed the requirements in the arduous apprenticeship program.

Gary Player was one of the critics, though he did so in a more diplomatic manner, expressing his sadness that a number of very good black players were being denied the chance to experience the great tournament because of very stringent rules.

The youngest winner in the history of The Masters happened to be the child of an African-American man and a Thai woman.

Tiger Woods finished 18 under par to earn his first major in 1997. Nick Faldo slipped the green jacket on his shoulders after Tiger embraced his father, Earl, in an unforgettable moment.

Tiger was a confident young player, not caring what anyone said about his game. He had worked hard to capture the Masters title, well aware that winning would not only be a massive achievement, but an electrifying declaration that he had arrived to take the PGA Tour by storm. His win transcended race. It was a story of hard work, spirit, pride and a father-son bond.

Woods was well aware of his place in history, but he was quick to credit Lee Elder, Ted Rhodes and Charlie Sifford as those who had paved the way for him. He had even thought about them the night before the final round and again while he was walking up the 18th on Sunday.

"I said a little prayer of thanks to those guys," Woods said and then added, "I think I understand why the big guy up in the sky has given me some of these talents, and I think the main reason is to help people."

Lee Elder cried tears of joy and admiration at Tiger's win, citing it as one of the most significant things he had witnessed in his life. Sifford was just as impressed, if a little envious, citing that Woods got to do what he had been denied.

At 21 years old, Woods said there was nothing better than having his parents share in his success and that his father's support and inspiration was the key to his winning the championship. President Bill Clinton, who called to congratulate Woods on his win, said that his favorite shot of the entire tournament, by far, was the shot of Tiger hugging his father.

Four years later, Tiger won The Masters again, cementing himself as one of the greatest golfers in the world because he had won four consecutive major titles in a span of 294 days.

On the final day on Sunday in 2001, Woods was three strokes ahead but missed a three-foot birdie putt on the infamous 15th hole. That allowed Phil Mickelson and David Duval to move into contention. Duval made seven birdies on his first 10 holes and two bogeys while Mickelson made clutch birdies at 8, 13 and 15 and they both moved within one stroke. But then the Tiger roared. He began to make almost every putt he needed, including the slamming-of-the-door birdie putt on the final hole.

Woods said that when he won his second green jacket, he experienced something he had never felt before. An eerie calm had come over him. The elation of winning was not like that in 1997. In 2001 he had a much deeper appreciation for what he had accomplished. He would make a staggering statement the following year in 2002 by winning again. Because Woods was a back-to-back winner, Chairman William W. "Hootie" Johnson was the one to put the green jacket on Tiger.

After a 10 no-win major drought since he won the 2002 US Open, Tiger was back in winning major form at the 2005 Masters. In the third round, he made up a four-shot deficit with only five shots over two holes in about 22 minutes. He then had seven straight birdies on his way to a three-shot lead going into the final round. On Sunday, he made the unforgettable shot on the 16th green where he made a sensational chip onto the green, using the green to run the ball down to the hole. The ball hesitated on the edge of the cup before dropping in dramatic fashion for a birdie. The roar was deafening. Going to the 17th tee, Tiger held a two-shot lead, but he sliced his tee shot into the pines, couldn't reach the green and bogeyed the hole. On the 18th, he bogeyed again and it forced a play-off with Chris DiMarco.

Previous sudden-death playoffs (since 1979) began at the 10th hole. This was the first time it would start on the 18th hole. Nothing could compare with what happened on the 16th in regulation, but still, it was a highly anticipated play-off.

Woods and DiMarco both put their drives in the fairway. Woods then knocked his approach to 15 feet of the hole, but DiMarco ended up just short of the green. DiMarco was able to knock his chip to within five feet, but Woods sunk his 15-foot birdie putt to win. The Tiger roared again. DiMarco slowly walked over to Woods and congratulated him.

The only thing lacking at the event was the man Tiger looked up to the most, his father. Earl Woods was too ill to attend the event. Tiger couldn't wait to get back and give his father a big bear hug.

Earl Woods died a little over a year later. It was the most devastating loss of Tiger's life and yet he was still able to win the 2006 Open Championship and the 2006 PGA Championship later that year.

A Masters' win can change the trajectory of a player's career, but a Masters' collapse can also make a significant impact on a pro. In 1989, Scott Hoch blew a two-foot-long putt to win the Masters in a play-off against Nick Faldo. As night fell on Augusta, fog saturated the course but Hoch's tears were clearly visible in the heavy mist. Though he had much success on tour, Hoch never won a major. He was further pained when later in the year he was voted as "Least Popular Golfer" by tour players in a poll conducted by a malicious Dallas newspaper.

Overall, despite the controversies, The Masters is a positive in the game. Each of us has our own memories of the event through the years, our favorite winners or favorite shots but few can argue that 1986 has got to be one of the best years in Masters' history. Even after all he had accomplished, that day in April when Nicklaus captured his sixth green jacket may have been his finest hour.

At the age of 46 and with zero wins in two seasons, his 7-under par 65, including a magnificent 30 over the inward half was as dramatic as it was difficult. Four strokes behind overnight leader Greg Norman, Nicklaus still faced fierce competition. Tom Kite and Seve Ballesteros (playing together) both holed long approaches for eagle 3 at the long 8th. Kite put more pressure on the other players with three birdies in five holes starting at the 11th, but missed a putt on the 14th that probably would have forced a play-off had he made it.

Ballesteros was like a loose cannon at times. A wayward iron shot went into the water hazard at 15 and then he three-putted the 17th. Norman also had an up and down round. A wild 4-iron on the 10th gave him a 6 for the second time in the tournament, but Norman regrouped with four consecutive birdies. Then the 4-iron betrayed him again on another hole. Norman pushed the ball into the gallery and failed to get up and down. Defending Champion Bernhard Langer dropped shots at the 7th and 8th and double bogeyed the last hole.

The notorious 15th hole played a part in the dramatic event once again. Still behind by four strokes, Nicklaus decided to go for broke. He knew he had to get there in two to have a real chance at winning. He stood in the 15th fairway looking toward the flag, squinting at the creek in front of the green. Nicklaus turned to his son Jack who was caddying for him.

"Do you think if I got a three here it would help?"

Jack Jr. smiled and handed his father a 4-iron. Nicklaus hit the shot. It flew 202 yards, landed on the green and began rolling in determined fashion toward the flag. It stopped 12 feet from the pin.

"Where'd it go?" Nicklaus asked.

But he never heard his son answer. The roar from the crowd was too loud. When he sank the putt for eagle three, the crowd went nuts. The sheer force of goodwill directed at Nicklaus seemed to lift him to birdie the 16th and the 17th. He was no longer behind by four strokes. He was ahead by one.

When Nicklaus walked up to the 18th green, his shadow was gigantic, casting his form completely across it.

"I couldn't hear a thing," Nicklaus said later.

He parred the 18th and waved to the crowd. He couldn't celebrate there because he had to wait for the other players to finish their round. One by one they came to the 18th green and failed.

Jack became the oldest player at the time to capture a major title. Nicklaus was obviously moved by the win. "It's been an unusual year for me," he said. "I only started playing well about a week ago. I thought this morning that if I shot 66 I'd tie, 65 and I would win and that's what happened. I haven't had this much fun in six years."

Nicklaus considered all of his major titles satisfying but said, "This one, at 46, in the December of my career you might say…" The words failed him.

Jack's win was a shock that reverberated throughout the world. He hadn't even been on the radar to win and some in the press even referred to him as "washed up."

Across America, people who weren't even interested in golf had their eyes glued to the television as a "middle-aged" golfer made a charge. There in the warm Augusta sunshine Nicklaus could hear the rumbling in the galleries and sense the collective will they had to see him win. The man with a steely nerve couldn't help but be touched by the support.

"Several times I started to get tears in my eyes and well up inside. I had to remind myself that I still had golf to play."

And play he did. Winning by one stroke over Tom Kite and Greg Norman the "youngsters" in the dusky light where Jack struggled with his bad eyesight, he had solidified himself as the greatest champion of all time.

Jack agreed the mental part was crucial. The previous week, a friend had put newspaper clippings up on the Nicklaus' fridge in the house they were renting. The clippings said things like "Nicklaus done. Nicklaus through. Nicklaus washed up."

A fire had been lit under Jack. How dare those writers who could barely break 100 mock Jack like that? But he was also fired up thinking about his mother, Helen. She had not attended Augusta since his first Masters' appearance and she had never seen her son win the green jacket.

All of these things were playing on Jack's mind and he answered back with skillful shots and defiant putting.

"For a guy who has won only $4,000 this year, this isn't a bad win," Nicklaus said at the ceremony, the largest crowd ever gathered for the trophy presentation.

Barbara Nicklaus, Jack's wife, said they never discussed whether his career was over or whether or not he would win another major. "I thought he could win another major if he would think he could win another major."

When the green jacket was placed on Jack's shoulders, he buttoned it, pulled on the lapels, smoothed the sleeves and smiled, satisfied.

The crowd noise was thunderous and people across the world have never stopped applauding for the son of Charlie and Helen Nicklaus.

CHAPTER EIGHTEEN

The Rivalry

The 1986 win at Augusta was the final major that Jack Nicklaus won – an outstanding 18 total major titles.

The achievements of Jack Nicklaus on and off the course are staggering – an example of a life lived with exemplary focus and determination. I never got to see Nicklaus play. I wish I had got to see Nicklaus play. Sure, I do enjoy watching some of the old TV footage of the tournaments Jack won but I never got to enjoy it while it was happening.

Over the years, different names have taken the title of important tournaments and majors, but no one has seen, can compare or can quite forget the brilliant showdowns and rivalry that was between Arnold Palmer and Jack Nicklaus.

In a ten-year span, Palmer and Nicklaus accumulated 14 major titles between them – not to mention all of the other events they won.

It is not to say that the triumvirate of Hogan, Nelson and Snead was anything less than fascinating, but something about Nicklaus/Palmer made for a good fight, particularly in major championships.

Palmer broke onto the scene in the late 1950's but he lacked a true equal until Jack Nicklaus turned professional in late 1961.

An amateur with a stunning record, the USGA was somewhat disappointed when Nicklaus turned pro. He was considered the finest amateur since Bobby Jones, but Jack insisted the move was not about money.

"I had much more of a chance to win the [US] Open as a professional than I would have as an amateur," he said. "Before, I was a student, a golfer and an insurance salesman and I could not spend as much time at any of them as I wanted. Now I've got nothing to worry about except golf."

The rivalry between Palmer and Nicklaus began from the get-go at Jack's first professional tournament – the 1962 US Open at Oakmont. The course had been softened by a deluge of rain, taking the edge off its sharp teeth.

"It's a break for a big hitter," pro Lew Worsham said after an early morning Wednesday practice round was cancelled due to weather. "The course will play longer but a man will be able to gun for the pin."

For the bronzed 32-year-old from Latrobe Pennsylvania, Palmer was looking to back up his Masters' win that April with another major win and he was the odds-on favorite. Most saw the chief competitor to Palmer as Oakmont itself, dubbed the "Hades of Hulton." Hulton was a nearby road.

1962 was the fourth time the US Open was held on the rolling hills of Pennsylvania steel country and at the time only one man, Ben Hogan, had broken par for the 72-hole route in 1953.

Oakmont had now been reduced to a 71 with a change in the 455-yard first hole. But 208 strategically placed sand traps, gnarly rough and glassy greens guaranteed Oakmont to be a monster. Many pros thought it would be tough to score better than 290, but Palmer disagreed.

"I've said before that I think 275 will win it and I still think so." As to the conditions, "I don't believe the rain has given me an advantage. I liked the greens as they were – hard and fast. I think they're the finest greens I've ever seen. The rain will make the rough tougher and it will mean that the greens will be chopped up for the late starters."

Palmer pulled the last stitch out of his ring finger of his right hand that he had split open earlier that week. "It doesn't bother me. Personally, I feel great. Never better."

For the opening round, Palmer was paired with the rookie Jack Nicklaus.

"I like the pairing," Palmer said. "I think the course favors a fellow like Nicklaus. He's stronger than I am. He can hit over most of the trouble."

Though most of the crowd was following Palmer/Nicklaus that first round, defending champion Gene Littler had the round of the day with a 69. At the end of the round, Palmer was tied for fourth and Jack Nicklaus stood tied for ninth having shot one over.

By the second round (still paired with Nicklaus) Palmer carded a 68 which put him in a tie for first with Bob Rosburg. Nicklaus shot a 70 and moved into a tie for fourth place.

Saturday was to be a long day with the third and fourth rounds to be played in sweltering heat. Palmer wobbled with a 73 in the morning with Nicklaus doing only slightly better, shooting a 72. Palmer was clinging to his share of the lead with fellow American Bobby Nichols. By the afternoon round, players were falling away and it soon became a duel between Nicklaus and Palmer. Palmer bogeyed the 9th, but was still leading Nicklaus at the turn. The score was evened when Nicklaus birdied the 11th and Palmer bogeyed 13. Palmer missed an 8-footer on the 17th and would need a birdie on 18 to win. Nicklaus missed his birdie attempt at the last and shot 69. It was now all up to Palmer.

Palmer drove mightily into the long grass to the left of the green and chipped to within 12 feet of the pin.

The crowd was salivating. All he needed to do was sink that birdie putt for back-to-back major wins, but Palmer hit his ball too firmly and it rolled four feet past the hole. He holed that putt to tie Nicklaus for an 18-hole play-off.

Palmer was rattled. He could not remember putting so poorly in a major tournament. He had 35 putts in the first round, 31 in the second, 38 in the third and 34 in the final round. He knew that was no way to win a tournament.

Nicklaus on the other hand was pleased with his game. "I only had one three-putt green," he boasted.

"Frankly, I wish it was someone else," Palmer admitted at the end of play on Saturday. "I thought I was through with him yesterday."

And how did Nicklaus feel? "I'm looking forward to playing Palmer," he said. "It's a privilege."

The massive crowd on Sunday was largely behind Palmer. Nicklaus was taunted by the gallery; no one seemed to care he was a young 22 year old playing his heart out.

Nicklaus had the match well in hand through eight holes, frustrating Arnie's Army. Palmer then went on to birdie 9, 11 and 12 to get within one of Nicklaus.

At the 13th hole, a 161-yard par 3, Palmer stood on the tee an extra moment debating whether to hit a full 5-iron or to take a 4-iron and try to hit a soft shot. He chose the 4-iron but didn't hit it well. His shot landed barely on the green about 40 feet from the pin. He then had an atrocious three-putt for bogey while Nicklaus got his par.

Palmer never caught up as Nicklaus was strong and steady the rest of the way, carding a 71 over Palmer's 74, to win his first major.

After the play-off, Nicklaus said that the 13th hole was where he got his big break.

"That's where I made my big mistake," Palmer groaned. "But I also three-putted the sixth hole and of course that hurt, but the 13th was my big mistake. I had a good shot at him after 12 holes and was in good position. I think if I had been able to stay within one shot of him there, I might have been able to make a better run at him."

"I didn't really think I had it won until Palmer missed his putt on 18," Nicklaus said. "But there's no doubt that I got my big break at 13. That gave me a big lift."

After Palmer birdied three out of four holes, Nicklaus thought Palmer was going to birdie three more holes, but it was not meant to be.

"It was my putting and chipping that did it," the new champion said. "I won it on those greens. I took my time putting. I didn't waste a stroke."

Nicklaus had recent experience with making three-putts at other events and he was not going to let that happen at the US Open. Palmer had been in a putting slump for three weeks and that continued into the major. He had 11 three-putt greens in the 90 holes he played including the last hole of the play-off when he made little effort to sink a meaningless putt for a bogey.

Someone asked Palmer if he intended on doing anything about his putter.

"I certainly do," he said. "I may quit this game or I may change my putter."

"That big strong dude," as Palmer called the youngster from Columbus Ohio who was 11 years younger than him. "He's a helluva player. He's got all the shots... everything. Time will tell but this young man is going to win a lot more championships." Palmer paused and in typical light-hearted fashion added, "I'm sorry to say."

It wasn't all accolades for Nicklaus, however. He was accused of being one of the slowest players in the game given the time he took to deliberate shots. He was the first known golfer to carry in his back pocket a chart of each course he played and he studied that book hard before each shot. For a man who could hit the ball further and more accurately than any player at the time, it was hard to find much fault with that, but the time he took over putts could just about drive his playing partner over the edge.

Then there was the matter of his weight. Early on, Nicklaus was considered "husky" by admirers and "fatso" or "well-fed" by detractors but he soon lost 30 pounds "just by playing golf." He also had definite swagger. He was confident bordering on cockiness. His swing off the tee or fairway was powerful but he made it look so easy and that aggravated more than a few people.

For Palmer, the US Open loss at Oakmont began a frustrating stretch as runner-up in 1963 (Boros), 1966 (Casper) and 1967 (Nicklaus). Backed by his loyal army (his galleries were twice the size of anyone), Palmer was even more emboldened to take on Nicklaus whenever they faced off in the final round. By the time of his final Masters win in 1964, Palmer admitted that win meant more to him than any in a very long time. He had been beaten on more than one occasion by Jack and it was wearing on the four-time green jacket winner.

Nicklaus tied for second place that year several strokes behind Palmer, but he appeared as confident as ever, claiming that he could have scored "five strokes or better" that Sunday. Anyone who had seen Nicklaus' tenacious game knew that was entirely possible.

Though the rivalry is over, the legacy of it remains to this day.

In December 2013 Jack and Gary Nicklaus played in the Father/Son PNC Challenge. All I wanted to see of that event was Jack play golf even if he was 73 years old. For those of us who know what Jack Nicklaus has meant to the game, you can appreciate how much fun it is to see the Golden Bear play at any age.

CHAPTER NINETEEN

On The Right Track

The last amateur to win the US Open was Johnny Goodman, the son of Lithuanian immigrants.

Goodman and his 12 siblings became orphans when their mother died while birthing her 13th child. The father abandoned the family and the kids were on their own. Johnny was 14 and began to focus more intently on playing golf. By age 16, he had his first win and it propelled him to other amateur titles. His 1933 US Open win at the North Shore Country Club in Glenview, Illinois would be the highlight not only of his amateur career but his entire golfing career. He did not turn pro until 1960, but his game never took off and he supported himself as an insurance salesman most of his life.

Watching young amateur players develop their game (particularly Woods) has been an extraordinary thing to watch over the last 15 years and the sheer number of talented juniors that have come up through the ranks is expanding all the time.

At one time, young Billy Mayfair was one of the promising upstarts, having won numerous junior golf tournaments before he was fifteen years old. He was stocky, blonde and fearless. He worked hard at his game and incorporated lifting weights into his work-out routine.

Mayfair started very young, at the age of two, with a set of miniature clubs. He played par three courses until advancing to regular municipal courses by the age of seven. Once he began entering tournaments, he was beating kids twice his age. He patterned his style after golfer Jerry Pate because Mayfair said he liked his style and his mother thought that Pate was handsome.

Mayfair had encouragement from his parents and his golf instructor and had a world of balance where he could work at his game and yet still be an honor roll student. His goal was to play on the PGA Tour, but as he began to travel, the exposure to what that life entailed took a toll on him. While playing at a Future Masters Tourney in Alabama, the humidity nearly crippled him physically as well as having to bat away hundreds of mosquitoes.

Mayfair may not yet have achieved the success he wants to date, but he does hold the distinction of beating Tiger Woods in a playoff on the PGA Tour at the 1998 Nissan Open.

Though few young players live up to the expectations of outsiders, we still get excited about a young golfer's game. I look at someone like Jordan Spieth and there is a mixture of envy and admiration. How did he get so poised and confident at such a young age? How does he stay steely-minded when playing with pros who have been on tour much longer than him, as evidenced by that final round of the 2013 John Deere Classic?

Spieth had been playing well but no one suspected that he would turn the tournament on its ear. In the final round, for his second shot at the Par 4 18th, Spieth found himself in the greenside bunker. He hit the shot well, if a little too much. His ball caught the flagstick and dropped in for a riveting birdie and a final round 65, but more importantly, it secured Spieth a play-off spot against Zach Johnson and David Hearn.

All three players headed to the 18th hole to determine the winner. Johnson and Spieth had good drives but Hearn hit his tee shot way right into the rough. His second shot was not anything to give him confidence as it ignored the green and found another patch of rough. Spieth landed his approach shot about 25 feet from the hole while Johnson just got it onto the edge of the green. Johnson collapsed to the ground as his brilliantly struck birdie putt just looped out. Spieth had a good look at the hole but came up two feet short. All players ended up making par and were sent back to the 18th tee.

Again, Hearn bungled his tee shot, landing again in the right rough. His second shot was well struck, finding himself set up well for birdie along with Johnson. All three players ended up making par before heading over to the Par 3 16th hole to continue the playoff. Spieth's shot came up short of the green while Johnson and Hearn both had good looks at birdie. It seemed over for Spieth, but both Hearn and Johnson missed their putts, so all men made par again.

The tension was rising. Who would win seemed an open question. On the Par 5 17th, it took Spieth four shots to make it to the green. Hearn laid a brilliant approach four feet from the hole for his birdie attempt. The hole denied Hearn the win by looping out his ball. Once again, all men had shot par.

By the 5th play-off hole, nerves were running high. They were back on the 18th tee and all the players missed the fairway. Johnson had a brutal lie behind an oak tree and ended up sending his ball into the water and eliminating himself from the play-off. Hearn battled to make bogey while Spieth came out victorious with a two putt par. It was a thrilling ride to witness the youngest player since 1931 to win his first championship.

Johnson almost got revenge weeks later at the Wyndam Championship. He was playing well and was in the final grouping on Sunday alongside Patrick Reed and John Huh but fell away. Spieth was lurking in the second to last group.

Reed was on track to win but gradually let a three-shot lead evaporate on the back nine on Sunday and found himself in a play-off with Spieth.

When they went to the Par 4, 18th first play-off hole, it looked like Reed was about to seal the deal with a birdie putt with Spieth having to putt 25 feet just to make par. Spieth drained the putt, perhaps rattling Reed because he pushed his birdie opportunity and had to settle for par and another play-off hole.

This time, it appeared Spieth had the advantage when he landed his second shot from a difficult lie seven feet from the pin. Reed's drive looked at first to be out of bounds, but the marshal signaled an all-clear and Reed found a miserable lie on some pine needles in the woods mere feet from being out of bounds. What happened next was what Reed called, "The best shot of my life" and what Spieth called, "One of the best shots I've ever witnessed." Reed gave it a good whack and landed it close to the hole for a short birdie putt. Spieth missed his birdie putt and Reed made his, handing him his first PGA tour win and denying Spieth the chance to be the youngest two-time PGA tour winner in recent time.

These are just two of the good young American players coming up, but all across the world, golfers regardless of race, creed or gender are shaping their games to take the world stage. Contrary to popular belief, this is not a new phenomenon. The game of golf was seeded in many countries long ago.

Back in 1903, a British Naval Officer wrote about his experience golfing in Weihaiwei China.

Weihaiwei first came into notoriety about 1898 at the conclusion of the Chino-Japanese War. Between 1898 and 1930, the city was part of the British-leased territory known as Weihaiwei or the Weihai Garrison and the city was known as Port Edward. Little did the combatants in the bombardment and torpedo attack on the port imagine that in the short space of eight years the then impregnable port was to become a favorite place to play golf by numerous British Naval officers and their guests.

Weihaiwei was a barren spot and full of "natural bunkers" – stagnant pools of water some 20 feet deep and 30 yards wide. Unfortunate was the golfer who could not safely carry such an obstacle as most caddies were not inclined to retrieve the ball.

Players also had to contend with a sloping and rocky course lay-out. Smack in the center of the course was a short wall that was the 500-yard firing range. Whenever there was a firing party using the range, hard and fast rules were applied to the golfer. If you sliced your tee shot, your ball was unrecoverable until the firing was over. Otherwise you had to hope an errant bullet wouldn't bite you because no one was going to yell "fore" as a warning.

One green was at the top edge of a precipice 100 feet in height. Many balls were lost there and expletives were flung over the cliff after them.

Putting greens were more accurately referred to as "putting gravel" because the holes were made up of hard-rolled sandy gravel requiring great care and constant attention. Approach shots were very difficult. A ball landing on the "green" inevitably over-ran the hole.

The officers employed locals to caddie for them, but the caddies spent most of their time trying to retrieve balls. It wasn't ideal conditions but if you could play a round of golf without getting shot and have at least one ball at the end, it was considered a successful outing.

Golf was not contained to Weihaiwei, China. One of the prettiest places to play was Deep Water Bay Links, a bay on the southern shore of Hong Kong Island. The greens on those links were worthy of the name. They were composed of excellent turf and compared favorably, in the opinion of some, with those at Hoylake and St Andrews. Hong Kong Island was beautifully wooded and the links lay in a narrow flat valley surrounded on three sides by hills covered with dense undergrowth.

The links were run under the auspices of the Royal Hong Kong Golf Club at Happy Valley. The trip to the course was a stiff ride over hilly rock-laden country so the majority of golfers playing at Deep Water Bay had to make an entire day of it even though it was just a nine-hole course.

Another nine-hole course was also getting play in Japan. The Kobe Golf Club was Japan's first golf course, built in 1903 by an English expatriate named Arthur Hasketh Groom.

Groom was energetically supported by several locals from Kobe even though none of them had ever played the game. Possibly as a credit to Groom's genial manner and enthusiastic expressions about the game, he was able to secure leases of the land from various village communities to whom it belonged and immediately set out mapping and cutting out a course of nine holes.

Development was not easy. The land was covered with stiff bamboo grass and undergrowth nearly three feet high and this had to be cut by hand more than once. In addition, about 6,000 azalea bushes were uprooted and in nearly every case earth was cut away to form greens – hardly environmentally sensitive planning.

The course was expanded to eighteen holes in 1904. Before the course even opened, it had already secured 95 members. About 100 people attended the opening ceremonies in perfect weather. Governor Hattori of the Hiogo Province opened the links by inexplicably driving off the first tee with a putter.

The vast army of men (mostly British) who arrived at the links did so in swinging first class carriages and were gently and freshly placed at the club house doors. In comparison, the local golfer had a more brutal journey on foot to the top of the mountain course.

On assignment to review the course, one writer named EJ Spurgin traveled by train to Kobe. There, he met a man who knew the way to the links and would carry Spurgin's clubs. The caddie wore a Kimono with an obi sash around his waist that held his pipe with a brass mouthpiece and a tiny brass bowl and bamboo stem with tobacco pouch. He wore straw sandals and bought another pair on the way up to Mount Rokko. He knew no English and Spurgin only knew two Japanese words: "river and temple gateway" both of which were useless for the purpose of this trip.

The links are situated on Mount Rokko about 2,500 feet high and five miles from the center of the city of Kobe. From the station to the top of the mountain was a very steep and tiring climb. The trail followed the course from a deep ravine where a shallow river ran, decorated by cascading waterfalls. Half-way up the path to the links, the caddie threw away his first pair of shoes and put on the second.

Pines covered the splendid gorges that led up the mountain from the sea. Spurgin paused often to catch his breath. To the west, Mount Rokko overlooked volcanic peaks right down to the misty islands. To the north were beautiful blue-tinted mountains of the most exquisite color and form and to the south lay the Bay of Osaka. The bay was crowded with men-of-war and gun boats that were continually arriving to take part in the Japanese Naval Review.

The magnificent view at the top of the mountain was great reward for the tiring five mile climb. The course itself had deep valleys, boulders, bamboo grass and a flaming mass of azaleas of all shades mingled with small maple bushes and stunted Scotch firs that made the terrain interesting and difficult. The "greens" were compressed gravel, mostly level. One hole was so well-guarded by a vast ravine, the fate of a shot would be unknown as the ball was likely never to be seen again.

Playing one of the holes, Spurgin was startled when he disturbed a beautiful lizard about twelve inches in length that shot away from him like a rocket. At another hole, he had to play the ball from a clump of pretty orchids.

On the climb back down to Kobe, the caddie pointed out a large building in the little village of Sumiyoshi that Spurgin assumed was a hotel. Spurgin went up, rang the bell and was greeted by an Englishman. It turned out it was actually a private residence, but the ex-pat invited the exhausted Spurgin in and refreshed him with a cold beer before he and his caddie made the five mile journey back to Kobe. All in all, it was a strange and mystical experience for Spurgin. The raw beauty of the course remained with him for his entire life.

The Far East was not the only region becoming attuned to the game of golf, but it usually stemmed from the fact that the English were bringing it to these other countries.

Baden-Baden is located in the northern foothills of the Black Forest in Germany where, at the time, Reverend White served as chaplain in the city. White had put his energy into developing a skillfully laid out golf course that was put under the care of a superintendent named George Dunn. Two of the putting greens were turf that was from a disused tennis court. The other holes were natural grass but were taking a long time to grow. Dunn said that when they did grow, they would be better than those at La Boulie in France. Hard to believe given that La Boulie had been built nearly 30 years earlier, but the superintendent had great dreams for his little course.

The holes varied in length from 120 to 225 yards and the bunkers were well placed to catch bad shots. On the whole, the course, though short and flat, was better than those that were cropping up in unusual places. The enlargement of the course was only a question of money as there was plenty of land adjacent to it.

The beautiful setting with views of an old abandoned castle and picturesque mountains also included an architecturally stunning pavilion that was just across the line from the platform to the train station but only members were allowed to cross that line.

Sadly, golf was developing into an exclusionary sport that would impact the game for more than a century.

CHAPTER TWENTY

The Importance of Golf

Commentators and fans often make comments about the millions of dollars golfers are raking in now that golf is big business. In the time of Hogan, Snead, Nelson, Nicklaus, Palmer and Player and many others, most of their income was earned off the golf course from endorsement deals, golf course design and other ventures. How times have changed. However, today, as it was then, a sense of giving back to the community has always been a part of the game. The PGA Tour has donated millions to charity not to mention the amount of charitable contributions individual golfers have raised through their own organizations and foundations. So maybe the next time you hear someone ignorant to the game of golf complain about it being a selfish game or unimportant or even boring, perhaps a mention of the significant impact the game has made in benefiting the lives of others can be asserted. As for boring, well, those who know the game understand that it is anything but boring.

Back in 1965, Gary Player gave the USGA an unexpected "problem" when he returned the $25,000 he won at Bellerive Country Club, St. Louis, Missouri.

The USGA was astonished and delighted when Player asked that $5,000 go for cancer research because his mother had died of cancer and $20,000 be set aside for the development of junior golf.

Giving away his champion's check had been on Player's mind since 1962. He was walking down the 17th fairway in the final round at Oakmont when he thought about how much he'd like to give away the winning check. Instead, Player finished five strokes back of Jack Nicklaus and Arnold Palmer that year. The next day, Nicklaus beat Palmer in a play-off.

Player was determined that when he did win another major, the championship check would be given away – and he did just that. The pro did not cheat his caddie out of the winnings, however. Player gave $2,000 to his bag-toter, a 16 year old boy named Frank Pagel.

Pagel said that his windfall would go towards a motorcycle and a college education even though he had not done very much.

"[Player] didn't ask me any questions. He knew all the fairways but he sure was nice to me."

1965 was also the year that Gary Player joined the small group of elite players who have won the Grand Slam. With Player and other pros helping others, it is why they deserve our admiration and respect.

The donations, contributions, events, and programs have elevated the game of golf to an important part of life in general. To be a young kid today with access to golf programs may have changed my entire life. Today it is no big deal for a girl to show interest in the game and golf is less thought of as an exclusionary sport.

Many times I felt excluded from golf. When I arrive at the first tee with Joe and we need to be paired with other (usually male) golfers, very few want to be paired with a female. I imagine it impedes the ability for a man to fully enjoy the game, swear, fart, let his guard down and I understand that. But I am not there to impede anyone's game. I take my game, even though it is recreational, very seriously. I have fun. I laugh, look around and cheer on others but make no mistake how much this game means to me. So when you see a woman or a kid or an overweight golfer or someone not wearing appropriate golf attire out there, don't automatically assume they will be a problem. They just might surprise you.

Above all, etiquette on the course is something we all could be reminded of again and again. Often, when I get to my ball, the other players race ahead of my ball and are directly in my view. Give your playing partners the consideration to not race ahead on the fairway, to not walk around and make noises on the tee box or the green. Ready golf is a good way to pick up the pace, but it doesn't mean etiquette is thrown out the window.

The other thing I have learned through golf is the ability to let go of bad shots and put golf into perspective. Our senses are more attuned than we realize. We have to give up trying to control everything. The human body is phenomenal, whoever "invented" it and we have all the reason in the world to trust that it will receive the message of what we are trying to accomplish and bring about the physical action needed to accomplish that goal if we maintain a practice schedule that contains sound fundamentals.

It took me a while to realize that setting realistic goals in golf is essential to progressing in this game. Before each round, I have just one goal. For a beginner that can be to just get every ball from the fairway into the air or to commit to each shot or for a more experienced player to make a certain amount of birdies. If you pile up too many goals or say "I just want to play well" nothing will be achieved. My goal often is that I want to hit each shot pure and results follow from that. Winging it in life doesn't work and neither does it in golf. There is a fine line between goal setting and expectation and managing that can be the most challenging thing in golf but it is doable.

Setting up that one goal and meeting it gives me tremendous satisfaction after a round. By building on these goals, my handicap has been whittled away slowly but surely. Being unfocused and aimless is not a good way to live life and it is certainly not good for golf. In my opinion, golf has a way of revealing how you live your life. Do you have goals? Do you put in the time and effort? Do you just want things without doing the hard work? Without meeting these challenges head-on, you (and your handicap) are going nowhere.

It's a common occurrence for any golfer to try too hard and want it too much. For me, I felt like time was running out. It took so long for me to be able to play the game and now that I was over 40, I felt that my best physical years were behind me and potential health problems in the future would curtail my ability to enjoy the game for the next several years. I have to remind myself that golf can be played for a lifetime and that is one of the great aspects of the game.

As to my parents, our relationship is tolerable. When I told my father about my hole-in one, he was delighted. "I can say that has never happened in our family before. Congratulations!" But he still believes golf is a waste of time. I don't accept that notion.

I love golf as much as I could love another human being. When I get to the first tee, I have tears in my eyes – not because I am insecure. It's because I made it there. Getting to play golf may be a simple accomplishment to many, but it is a huge accomplishment to me. Golf saved me in my childhood and it rescued me from the white-knuckle terror that is agoraphobia. Because of golf I have toughened up. It strengthened my mind. It strengthened my confidence and it strengthened my character.

Golf has made me a better person and I can't think of anything more important in life than becoming a better person – while playing golf along the way.

GOLF ETIQUETTE 101 – USGA

The Spirit Of The Game

Unlike many sports, golf is played, for the most part, without the supervision of a referee or umpire. The game relies on the integrity of the individual to show consideration for other players and to abide by the Rules. All players should conduct themselves in a disciplined manner, demonstrating courtesy and sportsmanship at all times, irrespective of how competitive they may be.

This is the spirit of the game of golf.

Safety

Players should ensure that no one is standing close by or in a position to be hit by the club, the ball or any stones, pebbles, twigs or the like when they make a stroke or practice swing.

Players should not play until the players in front are out of range.

Players should always alert green-staff nearby or ahead when they are about to make a stroke that might endanger them.

If a player plays a ball in a direction where there is a danger of hitting someone, he should immediately shout a warning. The traditional word of warning in such a situation is "fore."

Consideration For Other Players

Players should always show consideration for other players on the course and should not disturb their play by moving, talking or making any unnecessary noise.

Players should ensure that any electronic device taken onto the course does not distract other players.

On the teeing ground, a player should not tee his ball until it is his turn to play.

Players should not stand close to or directly behind the ball, or directly behind the hole, when a player is about to play.

On the Putting Green

On the putting green, players should not stand on another player's line of putt or when he is making a stroke, cast a shadow over his line of putt.

Players should remain on or close to the putting green until all other players in the group have holed out.

Scoring

In stroke play, a player who is acting as a marker should, if necessary, on the way to the next tee, check the score with the player concerned and record it.

Pace Of Play

Players should play at a good pace. The Committee may establish pace of play guidelines that all players should follow.

It is a group's responsibility to keep up with the group in front. If it loses a clear hole and it is delaying the group behind, it should invite the group behind to play through, irrespective of the number of players in that group.

Be Ready to Play

Players should be ready to play as soon as it is their turn to play. When playing on or near the putting green, they should leave their bags or carts in such a position as will enable quick movement off the green and towards the next tee. When the play of a hole has been completed, players should immediately leave the putting green.

Lost Ball

If a player believes his ball may be lost outside a water hazard or is out of bounds, to save time, he should play a provisional ball.

Players searching for a ball should signal the players in the group behind them to play through as soon as it becomes apparent that the ball will not easily be found.

They should not search for five minutes before doing so. Having allowed the group behind to play through, they should not continue play until that group has passed and is out of range.

Priority On The Course

Unless otherwise determined by the Committee, priority on the course is determined by a group's pace of play. Any group playing a whole round is entitled to pass a group playing a shorter round.

Care Of The Course

Bunkers

Before leaving a bunker, players should carefully fill up and smooth over all holes and footprints made by them and any nearby made by others. If a rake is within reasonable proximity of the bunker, the rake should be used for this purpose.

Repair of Divots, Ball-Marks and Damage by Shoes

Players should carefully repair any divot holes made by them and any damage to the putting green made by the impact of a ball (whether or not made by the player himself). On completion of the hole by all players in the group, damage to the putting green caused by golf shoes should be repaired.

Preventing Unnecessary Damage

Players should avoid causing damage to the course by removing divots when taking practice swings or by hitting the head of a club into the ground, whether in anger or for any other reason.

Players should ensure that no damage is done to the putting green when putting down bags or the flagstick.

In order to avoid damaging the hole, players and caddies should not stand too close to the hole and should take care during the handling of the flagstick and the removal of a ball from the hole. The head of a club should not be used to remove a ball from the hole.

Players should not lean on their clubs when on the putting green, particularly when removing the ball from the hole.

The flagstick should be properly replaced in the hole before players leave the putting green.

Local notices regulating the movement of golf carts should be strictly observed.

Penalties For Breach

If players follow the guidelines in this Section, it will make the game more enjoyable for everyone.

If a player consistently disregards these guidelines during a round or over a period of time to the detriment of others, it is recommended that the Committee consider taking appropriate disciplinary action against the offending player. Such action may, for example, include prohibiting play for a limited time on the course or in a certain number of competitions. This is considered to be justifiable in terms of protecting the interest of the majority of golfers who wish to play in accordance with these guidelines.

In the case of a serious breach of Etiquette, the Committee may disqualify a player under Rule 33-7.

Now, Go Play!